Letters from Paris

à Maria Cuecken

en souvenir du 4 mai 2010

A Halifax Lass Tackles the Sorbonne...
1954/55

Nancy Wickwire Fraser

Nancy ...ckwire Fraser

With original sketches by the author

Cover design and illustrations: Nancy Wickwire Fraser
Back cover photo: Susan Ashley

Library and Archives Canada Cataloguing in Publication

Fraser, Nancy Wickwire
    Letters from Paris: a Halifax lass tackles the Sorbonne...1954/55 /
    Nancy Wickwire Fraser; with original sketches by the author.

ISBN 978-0-9780700-1-4

    1. Fraser, Nancy Wickwire – Correspondence. 2. Université de Paris – Students – Correspondence. 3. Paris (France) – Social life and customs – 20th century. 4. Graduate students – France – Paris – Correspondence. 5. Graduate students – Nova Scotia – Halifax – Correspondence. 6. Canadians – France – Paris – Correspondence.
I. Title.

LF2209.F73 2008   378.44'361092   C2008-903585-2

Printed in Canada by Henderson Printing Inc., Brockville, Ontario

Table of Contents

Introduction

The French language entered my life at age nine. A bachelor gentleman named Ed Crawley, a First World War veteran, dined with us at our home in Middleton, Nova Scotia and to amuse me, he displayed the French he'd learned in the trenches: *un, deux, trois, quatre, cinq*...I was fascinated.

In 1946, we moved to Halifax. As a full program of French was compulsory for university-bound students, my classmates and I progressed through a heavy, grammar-translation course at Queen Elizabeth High School under the expert direction of Mademoiselle Blois (pronounced 'Bloyce'). Our text for Grades 10, 11 and 12 was Mathurin Dondo's so-called *Modern French Course,* published in 1930. Mathurin ignored Québec and based his program exclusively on France, its history, literature and culture. We all longed to go there. By graduation day none of us could hold a simple conversation in French but could we parse, read and translate! Neither the subjunctive nor the *passé simple* held terrors for Dondo initiates.

An epiphany occurred at Dalhousie University. Professors Paul and Suzanne Chavy had recently arrived from France to effect a renaissance in the French Department. They actually spoke and conducted their lessons, in French—and for the first time we learned to respond. The Chavys formed a *Cercle français,* which met weekly to sing songs, listen to *Edith Piaf* and *Les Compagnons de la Chanson* 78 r.p.m. records, act skits and produce *soirées* for our amazed parents and fellow students. When copies of *Le Monde* and *Paris Match* appeared on the classroom table I fell in love. So the French language was not confined to a university textbook! Here was current, comprehensible reading material which complemented the classical literature Paul Chavy brought so vividly to life. I surrendered to a lifetime infatuation with anything French, graduating in 1954 with a B.A. and, thanks to Professor Chavy, a French government bursary.

The bursary funded ten months' room and board at the Cité internationale universitaire de Paris, a complex of student residences on the boulevard Jourdan—plus tuition at the Sorbonne. I was expected to return to Nova Scotia a year later and teach French with authentic *élan* and the much esteemed Parisian accent. I, who had never studied away from home in my life, sailed off on a Cunard steamship to the city of my dreams. I was twenty.

Learning to speak fluent French was an enchantment. Living in 1950s Paris, while culturally rewarding, was exasperating on a practical level. Unlike some of my comrades who wheedled second-year bursaries or took positions as *assistants* in French lycées, I returned to Canada at the end of the academic year, equipped with international self-confidence and two Sorbonne certificates, ready to begin a career as a teacher of French. The ensuing years were punctuated by frequent visits to France, mostly in order to (as the French say) *perfectionner* my adored second language at various universities during the summer long vacation.

In 1992, while visiting my mother in Halifax, I found a beribboned cache of wrinkled, airmail envelopes with French stamps, addressed to her in my handwriting—letters mailed from the Cité universitaire forty years before. What a year that was! France in 1954 was still suffering the effects of World War Two, governments fell with regularity, refrigerators were viewed with suspicion, the métro reeked of urine and yet the cultural life was richer than anything I'd ever imagined. Would others enjoy reading my student experiences? Perhaps…so I edited the letters and handed the resultant manuscript to my husband and two trusted friends, Professors Peter Waite and Paul Chavy of Dalhousie University. All three provided valuable editing advice.

Several publishers considered—and rejected—the manuscript explaining that 'the time is not right for a light-hearted book,' so it languished in a desk drawer. After the successes of *Mysterious Brockville* and *Mysterious Brockville 2*, I reconsidered. Could I not publish the letters myself? *Eh bien*, here they are.

French Embassy and Consulate documents authorizing my bursary.

**AMBASSADE DE FRANCE
AU CANADA**

Ottawa, le 20 juillet 1954.

Je soussigné, Edmond BERNARD, Attaché Culturel adjoint
à l'Ambassade de France au Canada, certifie que M ademoiselle
Nancy B. WICKWIRE, 224 Inglis St., HALIFAX, N.S. (Canada)
est titulaire d'une bourse du Gouvernement Français pour aller
poursuivre ses études en France durant l'année 1954-1955.

Je serais reconnaissant aux autorités françaises de
toute l'aide qu'elles pourront lui apporter pour faciliter son
voyage et son séjour en France./.

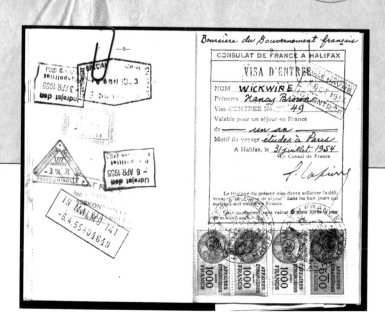

vi

"YOUR TRAVEL AGENT"

MEMBER

MARITIME TRAVEL SERVICE
76 Granville Street
HALIFAX, N. S.

CABLE ADDRESS
"MARTRAV"

TELEPHONES
2-4441
2-4442

May 17, 1954

Miss Nancy Wickwire,
224 Inglis Street,
Halifax, Nova Scotia

Dear Miss Wickwire:

      In accordance with your instruc-
tions we have requested tourist class accommo-
dation in the SS "Scythia," Quebec to LeHavre,
September 29th, 1954. The Cunard Line have now
offered berth 1 in Room M71, at a rate of $160.00
plus $5.00 French port tax, or a total of $165.00,
and they have given us an option on the above space
until May 25th. Will you therefore please be kind
enough to advise before that date if this accommoda-
tion is suitable and if so, we will require a deposit
of $30.00 in order to protect your reservation.

      Yours very truly,

   MARITIME TRAVEL SERVICE

nb.   Manager.

To
Professor Paul Chavy
1914 – 2003

APPRENTISSAGE

(the apprentice)

September 20 to December 22, 1954

APPRENTISSAGE

From **BRITANNICA BOOK OF THE YEAR, 1954**

SEPTEMBER

September 27: U.S. senate select committee unanimously recommended to the senate that Sen. Joseph McCarthy be censured on two charges.

September 28: Conference of the foreign ministers of Belgium, Canada, France, German Federal Republic, Italy, Luxembourg, the Netherlands, the United Kingdom and the U.S. opened at London to consider questions of west German sovereignty and rearmament.

OCTOBER

October 2: New York Giants baseball team defeated the Cleveland Indians, 7 to 4, to win the world series in four straight games.

October 7: Contralto Marian Anderson became the first Negro to be engaged by the Metropolitan Opera Co.

October 17: Pres. Eisenhower declared North and South Carolina a federal disaster area as a result of severe damage caused by the hurricane "Hazel".

October 23: Termination of the occupation of western Germany, its admission to NATO and the establishment of the Western European union were provided for in agreements signed in Paris.

October 28: Swedish academy awarded the 1954 Nobel prize for literature to Ernest Hemingway.

NOVEMBER

November 10: French cabinet adopted a series of measures designed to limit the manufacture, sale and consumption of alcoholic beverages.

November 18: (British) House of Commons approved, by vote of 264 to 4, the Paris accords on western Germany; most of the Labour party members abstained.

November 19: Canadian and U.S. governments announced that the U.S. had undertaken to build and finance a 3,000-mi. radar warning system across the Canadian arctic.

DECEMBER

December 6: Shah Mohammed Riza Pahlevi of Iran and his wife, Queen Soraya, arrived in New York, N.Y. for a two-month visit to the U.S.

December 9: Lawrence (Yogi) Berra was named most valuable player in the American baseball league in a poll of the Baseball Writers Assn. of America.

December 30: French National assembly voted, 287 to 260, to ratify the treaty creating the Western European union, including western Germany, and providing for a German army of 12 divisions.

I walk about Quebec

wave goodbye from the boat

get into my slacks

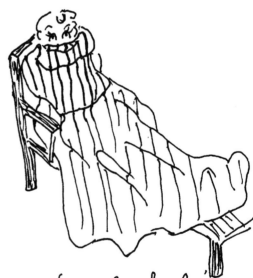

rent a deck chair

AND STAY THERE!

CUNARD LINE R.M.S. SCYTHIA

September 20, 1954

Dear Mom:

Ahem! How interesting this crossing is going to be! I'm afraid I was spoiled by having my first ship voyage on the Empress of France because the Scythia is several notches down. Examples?

- Man to wife, as we lined up for meal stubs: "Of course these are strictly immigrant ships, you know."
- No ship's newspaper.
- At a table for six, only two menus.
- The waiters bring juice and main course at the same time and whip your plate, knife and fork away as soon as you take your hands off them.
- The menu is limited and served without style: e.g. a mess of soupy, boiled rice slopped on a plate and presented as rice pudding.

Let's be more cheerful. I received a box of beautiful, long-stemmed roses, of a deep yellow and apricot shade, from my pals at the *Halifax Herald*.[1] Let me tell you how sophisticated I felt especially as none of the other three *wimmin* in the cabin got anything. I must tell you forthwith about my cabin mates.

I started off with two, both very British and named (naturally) Violet and Lil. As Lil is married I call her Mrs. Ashton. She has a most odd accent—sort of a combination Cockney and Brooklyn and is the original Dumb Femme. She pulled out her cigarettes and offered me one, which I refused. "Oh? You 'aven't started yet?" When I explained that I didn't like cigarettes, no, not at all, no, thank you anyway, she smiled a knowing little smile. I felt like a baby barely out of diapers. Then closing the door, she got out a bottle of whisky. She poured me an enormous slug and one for Violet. I sneaked most of mine into the sink and filled up my glass with water while Mrs. Ashton drank hers straight. Ah, life!

slug of whisky

Then Vi brought in another English woman whose name is Mrs. James and who looks like a very divorced divorcee to me.

She has a mauve nylon nightie, a satin housecoat, a perforated duodenal ulcer, a diet, shouldn't smoke (sigh). Mrs. J. moved into the top bunk and so we were four.

There ensued a scene in which I unpacked my suitcase, Violet, Lil and Mrs. James watching intently. At first there was silence.
Lil (disapprovingly): Aow, you've got two skirts to your suit, 'ow nice.
Me (apologetically): It's an English suit.
Lil (with satisfaction): I thought it looked good.

This morning Mrs. Ashton was looking for her 'bage' suit. After we finally understood that she meant 'beige', not 'bathing' suit, she worried about wearing blue shoes with it. "Oh, wear 'em," said the glamorously nightgowned Mrs. James from the top bunk. "Canadians don't care what colours go with what, anyway." She then smiled at me, a gesture which I received with extreme grace. Mrs. Ashton 'didn't buy a dress in Canada before coming aboard because in England she can get such nice things, that fit her, too'. I'm laughing. You should see her. She looks like this:

They're broadcasting the World Series now in the library, where I am. Since nearly the whole passenger list is British, I fear no one is listening.

There are a lot of mothers with children aboard, going to join their husbands in the air force, stationed in England and France; also a number of fellows who are being deported from Canada for one thing and another, mostly causing shipping strikes in Sydney and Montreal. A male passenger found one of these johnnies going through his locker one dark night. Gives you such a safe feeling, eh? I relayed the scandal to my three cabin mates who showed more eagerness than anxiety. Heaven help any man who wanders into our cabin!

My, I'll be glad to get on dry land. We've been rolling about and, though I haven't been sick, I sleep a good deal. Yesterday I slept all afternoon and all night from 11:00 to 8:30 AM and I'm still drowsy. Maybe I've got a tapeworm, heh, heh? Only that would make me hungry, wouldn't it and I'm not, especially.

Wednesday, 6 October

Today we passed the Scilly Isles (tremendous classroom joke) and Land's End. It's so exciting, I can hardly sit still. My three Limey room-mates, to whom I have never been able to warm up, are out partying just now so the cabin is mine alone—hah! (Mrs. J., she of the mauve nightie and the weak constitution, waltzed in at seven o'clock this morning. When I'm roused at 4:00 AM tomorrow (Le Havre passengers must breakfast at five) it will wake them up, too. I should be sorry, shouldn't I? Yes, I should.

Docking at Havre

Oh, I'm so excited. Do you suppose cousin Maria [2] will meet me at the *gare*? [3] I don't. My trunk, which travels separately, is being sent to les Batignolles, whatever that is, at a cost of two dollars. Hope I see it again.

Adieu and *au revoir* and *bien à vous*, Nancy.

[1] The Halifax *Herald* and *Mail-Star* were Nova Scotia's daily newspapers. I'd worked in the library section all summer.

[2] My gaily irresponsible cousin, Maria Waddington, was thought to be in Paris but could equally well have been in Southampton, Grenoble or Strasbourg. She was abroad on a one-year study program with the Adelphi School of New York.

[3] railway station

CUNARD WHITE STAR

BOAT TRAIN SEAT RESERVATION

2ND CLASS TO PARIS

CAR 22

COMPARTMENT 8

LABEL YOUR HAND BAGGAGE AND CLAIM IT ~~IN CUSTOMS~~ UNDER CAR NUMBER ON THE PLATFORM

PARIS, THE CITÉ UNIVERSITAIRE

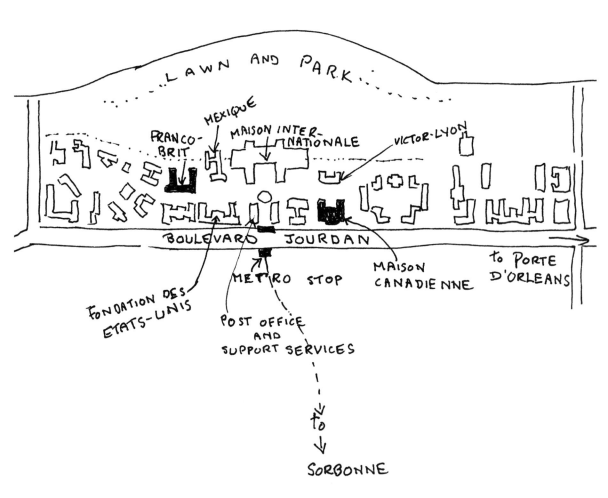

October 10
Room 102, Collège Franco-Britannique,
Cité universitaire, Paris

Dear Ma:

I address you from my room in the residence above, while waiting for some milk to heat. It's midnight here while you have just finished Sunday supper. (Going to check milk at end of hall. Pause while I drink my hot milk.)

Well. To begin at the beginning: after I got off the Scythia at Le Havre (pronounced 'Have-ree' by the English) I clambered aboard the train to Paris. It was a perfectly beautiful morning; pink clouds, blue sky. The trip to Paris seemed extra quick and the train rolled in around 11:30. Neither Maria nor Dorothy Yates[1] was at the station so I hoisted my two bags, coat and purse onto the nearest *métro* train. After much back-breaking heaving of suitcases, much asking for directions and changing lines I arrived at the Cité universitaire around 1:00 PM. I was, to be truthful, sort of scared, also hungry and my arms ached.

I stood frozen inside the gate for perhaps five minutes and finally addressed a boy who replied in American. He was most unhelpful really but did offer to carry my suitcase into the Fondation des Etats-Unis where I was told that the Collège Franco-Britannique was just across the path. I whipped over and asked if Mademoiselle Yates lived there? *Oui*, but *Mees Yatt* was not in. And before being assigned a room I would have to formalize my presence at the Comité d'Accueil office.

So, I went back into Paris on the métro and after much studying of maps, found the *Comité d'Accueil*[2] (96, boulevard Raspail). The people there were impatient and very rude, it seemed to me. My French deserted me and I think my English did too—it would have been funny if I hadn't been so close to tears. I was given some papers (at least they had my name) and told to return at *seize heures*, i.e. four o'clock. Fine.

I was starving by now so I trotted out in search of food. At a little restaurant I got the funniest ham sandwich—like a little loaf of French bread split in half lengthwise and the ham draped in between. It was hard to chew but tasted wonderful. Then I went into a bookstore where the people looked more helpful than the ordinary run of Parisians and got the man to contact the Canadian Embassy. The chap who answered was most cold and didn't offer to help me in any way. I could sleep on the sidewalk, seemed to be his song. Oh, Lord.

It being four o'clock I hied myself back to the Comité and met *Monsieur le directeur*, who ushered about fifteen of us, all new students, into his office and grilled each one separately. Every one of them, to my by then very flustered mind, could speak perfect French except me. It was awful, but I kept thinking, 'Well, Nancy, you have to do some unpleasant things in your life. You can't stay home forever.'

It was now 5:00 PM and I still had no bed for the night. Summoning the last ounce of French I possessed I tried to ask the secretary about my room. She was very busy and impatient and shuffled through a mound of papers while I tried to get across what I meant. Finally I turned away and burst into tears. I simply couldn't help it—when I tried to stop my whole body shook and I made horrible, choking sounds.

But…the change this sudden outburst wrought was miraculous! I was brought a cup of tea. A room at the Franco-Britannique was arranged for me immediately, my head was patted and I was invited to a cocktail party to be held the next day.

So, I went back to the Cité universitaire, got my room and found Dorothy Yates, who took me out to buy bread and cheese and grapes for supper. I was so grateful to have a roof over my head. My arms ached from lugging the suitcases, my feet hurt in high heels, I was hungry—but I HAD A ROOM. And believe it or not, I hadn't gone to the bathroom since five o'clock that morning. Quite a feat, don't you think?

My room is on the second floor and looks like this: My bed has a head lamp and bookshelves above it though the other bed has neither. I wondered briefly whether my occupying the better bed would be unchristian? But common sense overcame my more charitable motives. Just in time, too, for my roommate arrived the next morning. She came in, looked around, got out a pear and a knife, ate the pear, left and didn't reappear until Sunday (today). She then explained, in French, that she is staying with her cousin until Wednesday, so I'll have the room to myself for a while longer.

The meals at the Cité's student restaurant in the Maison internationale are fairly starchy, though there is salad (with lots of oil) once a day and meat and veg. And guess what—there are no napkins and we eat off tin dishes. The food is OK if you supplement it with cheese and fruit. There is a *crémerie* shop nearby which sells pasteurized milk and I crave it so, that I buy it and heat it up because I can't stand it at room temperature. Besides, I'm not quite sure that a second pasteurization isn't useful!

Dorothy introduced me to one of her friends, Monsieur de la Cruz from Ecuador, whose wife and children are in South America while he studies French. The day after I arrived he offered to help me retrieve my trunk. I was sure it was at les Batignolles as that's what the ship's porter said. We tramped for hours up wrong streets only to discover that *Non, la malle de Mademoiselle* was at the Gare St. Lazare. By this time I'd decided that Parisians (like those at the Comité d'Accueil) and adopted Parisians (like Monsieur de la Cruz) find it hard to stick to the matter at hand. For instance, I started off following M. de la C. like a puppy but soon found he had no sense of time or direction and I had to do most of the getting there myself.

After this I went to the Comité d'Accueil cocktail party and the following day, drew my October scholarship money. Francs at last!

Dorothy Yates took me to buy some crockery. What fun. The merchants display their wares right on the street outside their shops. It was chilly so Dorothy bought some roasted chestnuts in a bag to keep our hands warm. She showed me a *boulangerie* where you can buy Hovis, which is whole meal bread in a loaf shape and much more nourishing than the French bread.

It was Dorothy's birthday that night so she and I and Monsieur de la C. went to an Indo-Chinese friend's room where we had shrimp paste puffed in hot oil and a very rich, French cake which Dorothy cut with some difficulty because it was covered with a substance not unlike peanut brittle. Some white wine. French conversation. Two candles illuminating a dish of beautiful, translucent green grapes.

This morning I got up early to buy some breakfast stuff. Breezing into an *épicerie*, I asked for *"deux oeufs, une orange et un demi-LITRE de raisins"*. [3] Did I feel dumb? I meant a demi-KILO, of course.

This afternoon Monsieur de la Cruz escorted me to a museum in an old house where Madame de Sévigné [4] once dwelt and which contains a lot of info about the French Revolution. I'm going a lot of places with Monsieur de la C., yes? But over here it seems entirely different. Everybody pays his own way and is a buddy of everybody else, male or female, white, black, yellow or what-have-you.

I think I'm going to like Paris very much.

Good night! Nancy

[1] Dorothy Yates was Dalhousie's 1953 bursary student. She had decided to remain another year in France as an *assistante* in a *lycée* in Montauban.
[2] 'Welcoming Committee' (alias 'Trial by Ordeal'.)
[3] "two eggs, an orange and a half-litre of grapes."
[4] La marquise de Sévigné (1626-1696) celebrated author and letter-writer.

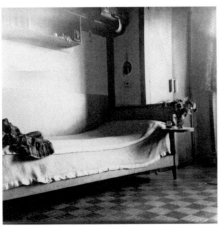

Room 102 'the better bed'

Dorothy Yates and Nancy on the Cité steps

Dear Mamma:

I got your letter this morning so I know you're wondering if I'm getting the proper food to eat and if I'm going to bed in good time and if I'm Keeping Regular with or without Eno's. Are you?

Here's the dope. Breakfast is available downstairs in the Franco at an outrageous price: coffee, French bread, butter, jam and fried eggs. As one pays separately for each item breakfast can cost more than lunch or dinner (which we students get at a great bargain for 75 francs, about 20 cents). I'm not fond of the French bread as it makes the inside of my mouth sore and besides, it can never fill me up and I seem to eat and eat and eat with butter and jam and so on—I'm sure it's not good for me—and it's quite hopeless without butter and jam. So, I buy oranges, pears and grapes and have fruit for breakfast with a slice of Hovis and cheese, sometimes honey, plus a cup of hot milk. Every other day, a scrambled egg (hotplate at end of hall, did I tell you?) and I have more hot milk at night. So you see, there's no need to worry. Anyone who does this is obviously conditioned, like Pavlov's dog, to stay healthy.

Thanksgiving night Dorothy and I and her Indo-Chinese friend, Dong Nouhé, went to a wonderful little restaurant near here (wonderfully expensive, too). It was a special occasion because Dorothy was about to leave for Montauban. We had chicken … and snails! I liked them. They are all doctored up outside the shell and then stuffed back in. You hold the shell with a thing like sugar tongs and dig the snail out with a little fork. With the chicken, potatoes *robe de chambre* which means 'in dressing gowns'. Isn't that delightful? A bottle of white wine and a lovely dessert of fruits mixed with a slightly rummy sauce.

Dear Dorothy has bequeathed me a glass tumbler and two male friends, Nouhé and M. de la Cruz. M. de la Cruz just loves to help people, Dorothy says. I found he was eager to go with me everywhere and, whenever we went into a shop, I would barely have my mouth open to ask for something and he would helpfully say it for me. My

French is far from perfect but I like to practise it myself—perhaps if I try and show how Strong and Self-sufficient I am, he will pick on someone else?[1]

And my own roommate, Simone (don't know her last name) occupied her bed for one night—Friday—but hasn't slept here before or since. I assumed she was at her cousin's but, on Friday afternoon, there was a letter lying open on the table. I picked it up. It began, 'My dearest love' and went on to say how happy the writer had been made during the last fortnight, etc. So goodness knows. And she looks very young, about 17. I noticed she's left a pair of sexy black panties and bra up to dry. Mercy! I'd expected to find myself very naïve and provincial when I got to Paris but I'm afraid I'm much more conservative than I'd ever dreamed.

Saturday I took a special bus tour to Fontainebleau, Versailles and Rambouillet. As a *boursière*[2] I got it all, plus a lovely meal at noon, for 400 francs—about a dollar fifty. It was a glorious day and the bus was full of boursiers and boursières of all nationalities: Canadian, South African, English, Egyptian, German, Turkish, Swedish, Bolivian, Argentinean, Brazilian—everything. And we all spoke French as a common medium. I was quite exhausted by the end of the day, not only from the walking but from speaking so much French and trying to understand so much more through fifty different national accents.

Last night I went to a *bal* at the Maison de l'Indochine with a Canadian student named John Clark, whom I'd met on the Scythia. It was a most frantic affair. Everybody was there: Egyptians, Arabs, Chinese and Africans plus some suave Latin types. The women were amazingly dirty and unkempt with stringy hair and skirts so tight you could practically see the goose pimples, or would have if it hadn't been so hot. I don't know where the ladies came from—I'd never seen them before. But I enjoyed it. Never have I seen such sexy, hippy Latin dances, never heard such screechy, Chinese and Latin American music. Golly. John Clark is a really short man who finds everything in Paris 'dreadfully amusing'. Despite the blasé pose, I was very grateful to him last night for his main virtue: he is **Canadian.** I'm glad I refused the invitations to the ball previously tendered me by a Frenchman and a Bolivian. Several very black fellows asked me to dance but I couldn't bring myself to accept. I guess I'm not ready for total brotherhood.

There are lots more men than women at the Cité, you see, so each female gets more than her share of unweeded, masculine attention. It certainly keeps you on your toes. I've found a marvelous defense. Whenever I don't want to answer an embarrassing question, such as, 'Do I bore you?' to which the answer is, 'Yes', I pretend I can't understand French. Sometimes, I must admit, I really don't.

3 GARÇONS pour 1 FILLE
From Journal de la Cité, 1954
a monthly residents' news sheet

The Cité universitaire is really beautiful with lots of lovely trees and lawns. Really, it's the nicest place in Paris to live; me, I'm used to my greenery outside the house, not squashed in a square in the middle of it. The chambermaids clean every day and rent, here at the Franco-Brit, is only 4,600 francs a month for a double room. Let's see…that's about 13 dollars a month. Imagine! At the Maison canadienne it's 6,400 francs.

But, you are asking, what about the studies? No classes as yet, only general orientation lectures called *conférences*. We had our first one yesterday. A little man with a moustache got behind a podium and raved for one and one-half hours, with thumpings, gestures, dramatic pauses and sudden, hair-raisings of the voice. I tried but couldn't understand a word. Oh, for dear, intelligible Professor Chavy! The second such *conférence* starts in 40 minutes so I'd better scoot. It takes half-an-hour on the métro to get there.

LATER

Surprise! We had an interesting lecture about the various university degrees in France compared to American and British Empire degrees. Canada was joyfully included in the Empire. This time I understood most of it—what a relief.

I've had to get what seems like a zillion little stamped cards, each adorned with my photo. The French love to make everything complicated, consequently I'm required to have individual cards to eat, sleep, study, draw my bursary and sojourn in France. I think I've got them all now except the various restaurant ones. These latter are, of course, the key documents and thus the most complicated of all to get. Therefore, on Saturday, I went to the special office to apply for my cards so that I could eat for 75 francs in any student restaurant. There are several near the Sorbonne so that one needn't go all the way back to the Cité for lunch. After being shunted from one bureau to the next, I was made to show my passport, scholarship card and *carte de séjour*[3] and received a small, yellow paper in return. I was instructed to go on Monday (today) to the *mairie* (which is 'mayor's office' in my dictionary, so I went there, only, surprise! it wasn't) and give them my small yellow paper. I did so and was given back the scholarship card and the two cards I'd filled out on Saturday. These I had to take back to the first office where a stamp was put on one of them, which cost me 50 francs. Whew! Now all I have to do is find the *Foyer international pour Jeunes Filles* which is the student restaurant Dorothy recommends.

Yesterday I went walking about the Cathédrale Notre-Dame and the Ile St. Louis with a student from Ceylon[4] named Sarasu. She was brought up in England but, unlike most English girls, is timid and lacks self-confidence. She is very bright, though, to make up for it.

I must stop writing or this'll cost me a fortune in stamps.

All my love, Nancy

[1] This must have worked as Monsieur de la C. disappears from my letters.
[2] bursary student
[3] residence permit
[4] now Sri Lanka

Some of the identification cards we students were required to carry at all times.
We also had to produce, on demand, our vaccination certificates and copies of our degrees.

October 22, Collège Franco-Brit

Dear Family:

Your letter came this morning. Poor Helen [1] and her horrid tonsils, especially after getting a lead role in the Q.E.H. [2] play. Now she'll have to have them out during Christmas holidays. What rotten luck. It's great of one to sympathize with another's discomforts when one is quite healthy oneself, isn't it?

Notice the use of the 'one'. It's a result of chumming with so many British girls. In fact I've even caught myself saying, 'Oh, jolly good!' and 'Not bloody likely!' If I return to Canada talking like this you have my permission to beat me over the head until I stop.

I have plunged into the live theatre scene by going to see *le Tartuffe* at the Comédie-Française (and I wouldn't have understood a word if I hadn't read it beforehand).The girl with the insipid, ingénue role made me giggle. It's the very part I'd have had to play if Dalhousie had staged it. I've found that understanding French speech let alone producing it myself is as sapping as climbing Mount Washington. I had to strain so to catch what the actors were saying that by the time *Tartuffe* was half-finished I was quite finished—and *tout à fait* exhausted.

I've met a frightfully nice English girl named Beth Ogilvie (Scottish, actually) who is teaching in a French *lycée* and rooms just down the hall. I don't want to speak English so much but just now I need the companionship more than the French language. French people, except for some leering males, are notoriously unfriendly. My roommate, for example, has only once essayed to begin a conversation. For one thing, I think she's miffed that I got the better bed.

Speaking of leering French males, let me tell you what happened yesterday. I had made a *sortie* to buy some biscottes which I shall explain to you right now. Biscottes are sort of slices of Canadian-shaped bread, thoroughly dried and toasted. They are hard and brittle but quite edible and keep for ages. Everyone English chortles at the very word 'biscotte' because we all buy them. Anyway, I had bought my biscottes and was strolling home when I heard the familiar, soft, *"Mademoiselle?"* behind me. These creeps always begin speaking while a few paces behind you and very gradually gain on you. I decided, for once, to practice the lingo, so I said, *"Hein?"* which he interpreted as an acceptance of his company. The ensuing conversation was in French. After a perfunctory opening gambit about what studies do you do and from where come you, he asked if I would like to come up to his room. I enquired if he were mad. Not to be foiled, he chivalrously offered to come up to mine. I politely replied that such things are forbidden. Would I like to promenade myself with him? No, thank you. Well, why not?

At that point I conveniently forgot my French and produced a flood of my native tongue whereupon he adroitly wheeled about, said, *"Au revoir"* and returned whence he had come. There is certainly no such species as 'secret admirer' around here.

The day before yesterday I walked all the way from the Cité to my Sorbonne conférence as it didn't begin until 5 PM. And oh! what fascinating little shops I passed! French window displays are enthralling. One china shop had wonderful cups and saucers, black outside and either deep pink or chartreuse or yellow inside; wrought iron somethings, modernistic glassware and stunning fruit plates and ashtrays. French blouses are fabulous and the gloves, purses and scarves put the water to the mouth (as they say here). Drool. As none of the above fit a student budget I bought a bunch of scarlet zinnias instead.

Last night Sarasu and I went to a French film called *Poison,* said to be a masterpiece. The French place much more importance on the director of a film than on the actors and the director of *Poison* was Sacha Guitry. Guitry (as we learned last year) is a Russian who devoted his life to theatre and finally to films. If only I could understand French better! Despite the title, it was a comedy and well-acted. There is a film every Thursday night at our own cinéma, here at the Cité— usually very good and always very cheap (90 francs, about 25 cents). Sarasu, incidentally, had trouble with the Comité d'Accueil too (remember my first day in Paris?) She has rechristened them '*Comité d'Hostilité*'.

I bought a hat today at Galéries Lafayette. It only cost 990 francs which is about $2.20, and it's black, very soft and slightly angora to the touch. It fits in the front and sort of folds in the back like an oversized beret. Feeling full of beans, I decided to have my hair cut, so I went into the first *coiffeur* place I saw and they did it immediately for 350 francs which included the tip. Then to compensate for loss of hair, I went into a café and ordered a *cascade*, which is an ice-cream wedge with fruit in it. It tasted yummy. My first Paris ice-cream, haircut and hat!

I was talking to Dorothy's Indo-Chinese friend, Nouhé, tonight. He is in such a difficult position. His family is in Indo-China [3] and being non-Communists, were forced to move from the North to the South. As Nouhé is certain that the Communists will eventually control all of Indo-China, he doesn't know whether to go home, where he could do nothing, or stay here and worry about it. His parents would be forced into exile—goodness knows where they would go—if the Communists take control. The easiest thing for the family to do would be, of course, to embrace communism, but they don't want to. It all seems incredible to me, coming from a country where no one would dare profess communism openly.

Yours most respectfully,
N. Wickwire (student)

[1] Helen, my younger sister. The play was *The Winslow Boy*.
[2] Queen Elizabeth High School, Halifax
[3] now Vietnam

COMÉDIE FRANÇAISE

SALLE RICHELIEU

Dear Family:

I have just finished my luncheon and now am a picture of pastoral serenity, sitting on the lawn behind the Franco-Brit, while the sun shineth so strongly that I am jacketless. I can hear the birds singing afar off (as the poets say) which is just as well, birds being birds and me with trees over my head.

The leaves are falling liberally now though most of the *arbres* are still covered in greens and yellows and browns. Please look at the November page of *Les Très Riches Heures du Duc de Berry*[1] in our LIFE book and you will see a swineherd, some pigs and some very tightly-packed, russet-leaved trees. I had always thought the painting an extreme stylization, but it's not. That's exactly what Paris' trees look like.

I went over to the Maison canadienne this morning for a cooked breakfast of oatmeal porridge, called *soupe* by the French. To sweeten it, the server drops in lumps of beet sugar and stirs. There I chatted with an English Montrealer whom I'd met on the trip to Versailles. He says his parents send his monthly allowance through the mail by buying French francs in Canada (it's cheaper to get them there, he says) and mailing them to him in a registered letter. Sounds risky to me. I think we'd better stick to the Royal Bank deposit plan though so far, the Royal's branch in Paris claims to have received no $35.00 deposit for me??

Our introductory lecture series finished this morning and now, we students must play a guessing game called 'When do the real classes begin?' It's all pretty disorganized. Last Tuesday I managed to inscribe myself in my course after having tried to do so on Monday and been instructed severely to return the following afternoon at 3:00 PM. I arrived on the dot of 2:55 only to find scads of students lined up ahead of me. By 5:30 it was my turn. I was led into the inner sanctum wherein Mlle Marin, *Directrice des études*, doth preside, and sat down. She officiously chose for me the same course Professor Chavy and I had selected months before and then announced that I would have to sit an exam on Tuesday next. 'An exam? On what?' 'It is to see how much French you know'. Save us Mrs. Davis! What if I have to explicate a passage from Voltaire? Fortunately, as Sarasu says comfortingly, since we have scholarships they can't very well send us home even if we flunk. Such is the romantic student life in Paris.

To return to this morning's lecture: a mad hatter of a professor raved away about *la liberté de Paris* for an hour. He's quite right in one sense, because over here you need report to no one on your activities (witness my roommate). You can skip meals and classes and stay out all night. Girls can wear slacks to classes and even to dances! Anyone can, and many do, roam the streets in full Highland dress or in a sari (Sarasu often does) or in Arabian robes and no one seems to raise an eyebrow. But dear me, let's look at the other side of the coin. For a city so enraptured by liberty Paris is entangled in the most elaborate maze of rules and regulations ever devised. We have to show a card every single time we go for a meal at the Cité restaurant. We require a *carte de séjour* just to breathe French air. Every wicket conceals a *fonctionnaire*[2] who demands our birth certificate, our passport and a copy of our degree. Involved rules glare from the windows of the métro. The ones I like best are:

> '*These benches are reserved:*
> *for those wounded in battle,*
> *for those injured in state work,*
> *for pregnant women,*
> *for women accompanied by children of less than four years.*'

and

> '*Because of work along the line, certain trains are susceptible of being slightly retarded.*'

Last Sunday I went on a solemn and dutiful pilgrimage to the Louvre, dressed handsomely—I thought—in my grey suit and new haircut. The usual crowd of Americans stood in reverence before the Mona Lisa as the usual art student beavered away on a copy (rather wooden). After walking slowly around, I sat down on a worn, velvety bench overlooking the Arc du Carrousel and, almost at once, an

English laddie approached and asked if I were American? Ah, Canadian! And like the Ancient Mariner, he launched into his tale of woe. He is a bank clerk from Bristol who, for his annual holiday, had gone to Bordeaux to pick grapes for the *vendanges*. There he and his fellow Brits had been treated like the lowliest of serfs. The overseer was a real baron who lived in the château. I thought that sort of thing died with the Revolution. At the end of the grape harvest, the French field hands ceremoniously presented the baron with a bunch of flowers and were each given, in return, a tot of rum and a biscuit. It all sounded awfully mediaeval to me and it was clear that the bank clerk was disgruntled over the way he'd spent his holiday. Could he take me out to lunch? No? To dinner, then? I refused politely and gazed earnestly at the traffic careening about the Arc below. Finally he left. One can pick up more than art in a museum.

Last Sunday, Sarasu, Kaye Leslie (Canadian), Beth Ogilvie and I headed to the Comédie-Française to see the matinée, *le Misanthrope*, a Molière classic. Since it was drizzling and unfit for promenading about, all of Paris had the same idea and consequently we couldn't get seats. While we were deciding what to do instead, the heavens opened and rain descended in sheets and pillowcases. So we returned pell-mell to the Franco-Brit, wet and breathless, and I invited everyone to my room for tea (as usual, my roommate was out). Kaye contributed some Nescafé, Sarasu and I, cookies, and Beth, a lovely fruitcake her mother in Scotland had sent her—plus the inevitable biscottes. Since it was pouring rain, we read aloud Somerset Maugham's short story, *Rain*, taking turns. I was the only one who'd read it before and even so I found it engrossing.

I bought some plum jam the other day. (♪What do we want with eggs and ham, when we've got plum and apple jam?♪)[3] The French make excellent jams and marmalades, really good, as if they were home-preserved. I wish I could send some to you but I think it's forbidden to mail food out. Maybe I shall smuggle some inside my trunk next July.

Last night I had just put on my slacks to go and have supper at Ye Olde Cité restaurant when the buzzer in my room rang. I hurried downstairs and there was Nouhé, who wanted to know if I would like to go out for a Chinese meal? Would I! (paying my own, of course.) Off slacks, on suit and away we ran to feast on Chinese ravioli soup, and rice and shrimps and duck and a Chinese salad and tea. Oh, I was so full and it was so delicious. Nouhé ate with chopsticks and I tried but reverted to knife and fork in barbarous Western fashion.

Love and kisses to you all (urp!) Nancy.

[1] A sumptuously illustrated 15th century calendar, reproduced in LIFE *'s Picture History of Western Man (1951)*
[2] civil servant
[3] World War I ditty

Nouhé–impeccably dressed as always

October 29

From a letter to Duncan [1]

....I've just come from lunch at the Maison internationale and on my way out, stopped to buy some more meal tickets. An English chap and his wife, obviously newly-arrived, were in the queue ahead of me. He turned around and asked me in nervous and slightly inaccurate French, "*Pourquoi, uh, ce queue?*" I replied in my best nasal tones that it was to buy the tickets for the meals. I then switched to English in order to explain more fully and they gazed at me gratefully. "You

[1] Duncan Fraser, whom I married two years later, was an articled law student.

speak English very well," said he. "Thank you", I replied modestly. So you see, I progress!

FASHION REPORT

French women are very smartly dressed. A great variety of hairdo's from crops to pigtails plus lots of long, tangled manes, dyed red or yellow. Flat shoes, low-belted coats and narrow, stovepipe slacks which look very neat. The young men of Paris are also doing their 'hairs' in the latest modes. Here is an on-the-spot report direct from the boulevard St. Michel, where your observer has noted two predominating coiffures. One is a sort of Julius Caesar thing, for which all the hair is combed straight out in all directions from a point in the crown, like this:

The other style is much more elaborate. It necessitates hours at the hairdresser's and looks something like this:

And that is not all. There is also the beard, which everyone grows as soon as he gets here and which can take many glorious forms, viz:

He who has no beard must content himself with a moustache.

Beth and Sarasu picnicking in the St. Rémy woods on November 1, le Jour des Morts *(we had a holiday).*

November 7

Dear Helen:

Last evening at about 6 PM I came huffing into the Collège Franco-Brit, having been out for a walk in chilly, misty Paris and simply longing for a cup of tea. Lo and behold, there was a little grey letter in my box and it was from you, *meine Schwester*. I drank my tea and had a letter to read while I drank it. Thank you very much!

Speaking of tea, etc., we are strictly forbidden to have electric hotplates in our rooms, so of course I've been simply dying to have one to cook on. The other morning I shelled out 875 francs for an element and cord and sneaked the ensemble home. I plugged it in; at once the fuse blew and all the lights went out. So, I went to the *concierge* and complained that the *lumière* didn't *marche* (saying nothing about the hotplate) and he had it fixed. Nothing daunted, I waited until I was quite ready for bed late that night, and plugged 'er in again. Zap! The lights extinguished themselves with a vengeance and this time the darkness was final. Rats. The next morning I smuggled the element out by wrapping it in a magazine and after a lot of stubborn haggling got the store to take it back. (You have to be firm in this country.) The worst part was asking the concierge again to fix the lights. Fortunately he's blind in one eye and can barely see out of the other so I don't think he recognized me.

My honest-to-goodness real classes begin tomorrow, just when I'm getting used to a life of indolence. Here is my schedule:

Monday: 8:30 'til noon: Vocabulary; Conversation; Geography.
Tuesday: 8:30 'til 4:00: History of Art; Vocabulary; Conversation;
Composition
Thursday: 8:30 'til 4:00: History of Art; Grammar; Literature
Friday: 9:45 'til 12:30: Vocabulary; Conversation; History.

It will sound slightly less terrifying if I explain that I only go to two of the Vocabulary and Conversation classes. I don't know yet which two.

Did you have lots of kiddies at the door for Hallowe'en? Nobody goes around for 'shell-outs' here, it's not celebrated in France. We

Canucks had our own little celebration last Saturday night in Kaye Leslie's room with a half-bottle of Martini and a jack o'lantern I had hollowed out of an apple.

9:45 PM. We had a first practice for Christmas carol singing this afternoon in the basement of the Franco-Brit (French and English carols in equal proportion.) Quite a few students turned up and they were reasonably orderly which surprised me. I seated myself beside a girl I'd not seen before who wore her hair in straggles behind her ears, no makeup, a shapeless black suit and oxfords, also black. She was English (of course) and is writing her doctoral thesis so is very brainy. When I asked her the subject of her thesis she sort of sneered, as if to say, 'You poor Colonial, what do you know about anything?' and finally replied, "Eighteenth-century literature"; and as I must have looked amazed, this being a rather wide subject for a thesis, she added tersely, "in general".

After this rebuff, I met a very nice English girl named Elizabeth Wade and invited her up to my room afterward for a cup of tea and a biscuit (not a biscotte!).

I'm speaking a lot of English but there seems to be no remedy except to snub all the friends I've made. Having the French roommate would help if she weren't out so much. This morning at the ungodly hour of 6:30 she got ready to go on a few days' holiday to Lyon and Geneva. I wonder if she might be, as they say delicately, 'in trouble'? She does look a bit tubbier around the middle. Why else would she leave just as term is beginning?

Now it's bedtime. I've just showered and washed my *cheveux* and got into my pyjamas, all prepared to meet that 8:30 AM deadline tomorrow. Somehow, as Elizabeth says, it takes a whole extra hour to prepare for an eight-thirty class: a nine o'clock class is a breeze in comparison.

> *Amour, amour et amour,*
> (one for each of you),
> Nancy

P.S. I went with Kaye to see *Porgy and Bess* last Sunday afternoon, presented by an American company; and it was wonderful. I confess I didn't know that *Summertime* and *It Ain't Necessarily So* and *I've Got Plenty o' Nothing* were from this opera. I enjoyed it to the hilt.

P.P.S. Duncan has sent me a couple of Dalhousie *Gazettes*. What a treat! Poor Graham Day [1] is still writing angry letters to the Editor, it seems.

---

[1] Sir Graham Day was a Q.E.H. and Dal. classmate. Our class predictions did not include his being knighted by the Queen in 1989 and appointed Chancellor of Dalhousie in 1994. 'Poor Graham', indeed!

13 novembre, afternoon

Dear Mamma:

Today is a lovely day—a simply heavenly day. Why? Because someone gave me a special *carte* enabling me to stand at the front of all queues? *Quelle blague.*[1] No, nothing special has happened, just a lot of little things put together. In the first place, the sun 'is shining with all his might' on the tree outside my window, covered with brilliant yellow and tawny leaves (and which, as Beth says, still conceals us from the sex-starved Mexican males in their Résidence next door). In the second place, it's Saturday, so I didn't have to get up until I chose to. Thirdly, my roommate was actually here, having come back last night from a trip to heaven-knows-where but—hooray! She went out again for the morning. Fourthly, after two fizzled attempts, I have successfully completed a *rédaction*[2] with the daringly original title *mes premières Impressions d'une Ville française* and, lastly, the buzzer rang, so I rushed downstairs to find Marc-Antoine, John Clark's French-Canadian roommate, who invited me to the *grand bal* tonight at the Maison internationale. And, oh yes! I got a letter from cousin Maria this morning—she is now in Grenoble—and I'm invited there for Christmas. Grenoble is right in the French Alps and we are going to *faire du ski*, Maria says. Whoopee!

In a few minutes I'm going half-way across Paris for a Saturday afternoon orchestral concert and tomorrow evening, Kaye Leslie and I are going to see *le grand Ballet du Marquis de Cuevas* at the Théâtre Sarah Bernhardt. I'm to meet her in the lobby as she'll be babysitting for a French family all afternoon.

MONDAY AFTERNOON REPORT

At the Saturday concert I was given a seat right under the feet of the conductor. Imagine being so close to a man named Ciril Cvetko! It did give me a chance to observe the musicians' faces, especially the one who played the piano in the Schumann concerto (and who clearly hadn't practiced enough).

After this, and full of music, I leapt on the métro, shot home, squeezed into the dining room just before it closed, gulped my supper and ran to my room to prepare for the bal. Would I look overdone in the black jersey *ensemble* with the rhinestone-besprinkled top and fuschia petticoat? *Non*, because it was a very elegant bal in a perfectly lovely ballroom (the Maison internationale was established by Rockefeller). There was a decidedly rhythmic dance band, the musicians sported long, ruffled sleeves, there were little tables at which to sit and everything. Marc-Antoine is one of those rare males who loves to dance and so I was whirled around and around until 1:30 AM when I decided I simply had to go home and unwind my insides. Parisian dance bands love to play and there are **no** intermissions. Can you imagine dancing solidly for four hours? Nor can I. But I did it!

Then Sunday evening, it was off to the ballet. I had a bit of trouble finding the Sarah Bernhardt theatre because I'd exited at the wrong métro stop so, approaching a skinny prostitute with dyed blond hair and a brilliantly painted face, I enunciated, "*Madame, je cherche le théâtre Sarah Bernhardt*". She stared at me, put her ear next to my mouth and said, "*HEIN?*" I repeated, slowly and in a gradually worsening accent, what I'd said and she jerked away her ear, made a face as if in great pain and shrieked, "*EEEEOOOOW? E-HEE-MOOOW?*" I rapidly concluded that as far as she was concerned, I was speaking Congolese. Anyway I was a bit scared so I slipped into an *épicerie* whose clerk kindly explained how to find the Sarah and I almost ran there, finding Kaye waiting patiently.

The *placeur* looked at Kaye's and my tickets and said indulgently, "*Par ici, mes enfants*".[3] We laughed and started up—and up—our seats were right next to the ceiling! But to compensate, we had a rail on which we could lean our elbows and look rapturously down, as those arty types do in the film *les Enfants du paradis*.[4]

Afterwards we walked over to the Seine to see the lights reflected in it and feel the cool, wide air. I felt as if I were in a dream. Back home, Kaye and I made café au lait and she produced two little pieces of chocolate cake with chocolate icing which the cook at the place where she babysits gave her. The first chocolate cake I've tasted in one-and-a-half months. It was delicious.

I've met such a pretty Irish girl named Jane Henry,[5] whose room is across the hall. She dresses very smartly which is unusual for a Britannique—of course the Brits are the first to admit that they are dowdy, I think they're proud of it. Anyway, as tomorrow evening the Scottish students are organizing a second evening of Scottish country dancing, Jane and I are going to go. I went last week and it was oodles of fun—it's like very refined square dancing.

Oh! My examination *placement* results have landed me in *groupe 2* (which is very good: *groupe 1* is the top).

Lots of love, Elder Dotter

P.S. If you send me any parcels I think you'd better register them. There is a lot of pilferage here.

P.P.S. The radio has just announced that Mendès France is to visit *Mac-Jeel* university during his trip to Canada.

---

[1] What a joke
[2] essay
[3] usher: "This way, children".
[4] Marcel Carné's iconic 1945 film. *Le paradis* is the topmost balcony in a theatre, i.e. 'the gods'.
[5] Jane had worked with Sibyl Connolly, the Irish couturière. That explained the classy wardrobe.

November 15

From a letter to Duncan

…. Kaye Leslie and I went to see *le grand Ballet du Marquis de Cuevas* but really, I was a bit disappointed. Halifax is no Paris but I've seen better ballet there. My problem with the Marquis is, that his *corps de ballet*, instead of being a corps, is divided into *plusieurs personnes*,[1] each of whom has his or her idea about when one should leap into the air or wave gracefully the arm. I certainly believe the French are the most individualistic of races. Beth says that when Sadlers Wells ballet came to Paris, the critics grudgingly noted that they had *précision* as if it were some kind of fault.

There is a perfectly corking book out (there I go using British slang again) called *les Carnets du Major Thompson*[2] which **all** the French and **all** the English people in France, are reading. The apocryphal Major, supposedly a retired Brit who lives in France, slices up both nationalities with hilarity. For example: *La France est le seul pays du monde où, si vous ajoutez dix citoyens à dix autres, vous ne faites pas une addition mais vingt divisions.*[3] I wonder if he's referring to the corps de ballet?

[1] several persons
[2] Daninos, Pierre. *Les Carnets du Major Thompson.* Paris: Librairie Hachette, 1954
[3] 'France is the only country in the world where, if you add ten citizens to ten others, you make, not an addition, but twenty divisions.'

THÉATRE SARAH BERNHARDT

Administrateur général	Directeur : A.-M. JULIEN	*Secrétaire général*
NADINE FAREL	SAISON 1954-1955	FRANÇOIS MAISTRE

GRAND BALLET
DU
MARQUIS DE CUEVAS

Directeur Général : MARQUIS DE CUEVAS
Maître de Ballet : BRONISLAVA NIJINSKA

Despite Bronislava Nijinska, sister of the great Vaslav Nijinski, the performance lacked éclat.

20 novembre, 10:00 AM

Dear M. and P:

Thank you for your letter and I'm so relieved, Mamma, that you got your birthday gloves. They weren't registered and I've been having visions in which a crafty postal assistant traipses out of her office wearing them. By the way, the peculiar numeral on the glove box is a 'one'. You see, French people write their '**1**' like this: Then they have to put a stroke through the '7' to distinguish it from the '1'.

Yesterday morning's educational feature was the big re-opening ceremony at the Sorbonne. All kinds of honorary degrees were awarded, including one to Dr. Wilder Penfield. President Coty was in attendance, trailed by a small army of press photographers plus movie and television cameras. It was pretty impressive even though I couldn't understand all that much of what was said.

And now…this week's news, reporting to you from where it is that I am (my bedroom):

ITEM: A cocktail party for all Canadian students was thrown at the Maison canadienne yester-evening. Let me tell you the best feature of the cocktail party. There was a fireplace with a wood fire burning in it. I was drawn to it like iron filings to a magnet and was pried away only with difficulty. (They seemed to be burning pieces of broken furniture. I hope no-one slept on the floor last night, having sacrificed his bed to the Cause!) After this, a bunch of Canadian maidens floated across the courtyard to the Maison internationale for dinner. If you could see the restaurant there you would realize what an anti-climax it is to cocktails. By the way, the Maison canadienne is for males only; Canadian females must rent rooms at the Franco-Britannique. I am told that this is to discourage immorality among the True North Strong and Free.

ITEM: I've met a charming French girl named Nicole Pouzargues who is studying for her Master's degree in English. She was sitting opposite me in the *Foyer international pour Jeunes Filles* and we had such a nice conversation, extended by a cup of café *filtre* at a proper restaurant later. We've exchanged timetables so that we can meet often and alternate French and English conversation. It really is worth it—making an effort to speak to people. We had coffee again yesterday.

ITEM: Colin Bergh from Dalhousie (remember him as Sisyphe in *Sisyphe et la Mort?*) wrote me from Amiens where he is an *assistant* in a lycée. Dorothy Yates and I had started to wonder if he were dead or alive!

ITEM: I have bought a red and black scarf to go with my red and black jersey dress. It was outrageously expensive and, to crown my wastrel afternoon, I also bought a red straw basket which is now on my table with an orange in it. It looked even nicer yesterday with green grapes and a tomato (since eaten).

BIG, BIG ITEM: My taciturn roommate has found herself an apartment and is moving out by degrees. She will be gone, lock, stock and barrel, by Monday and I will get someone else. I wonder who?

LAST ITEM: My phonetics teacher congratulated me on my pronunciation and asked me if I had an ear for music. So you see? I must be making progress. It just seems so s-l-o-w.

Love, Nancy

The Poor-house,
Paris XIVe, 22 novembre

Dear Daddy:

After merrily spending my last November centimes on such frivolities as flowers and yellow candles, I trotted off today, flat broke and having had neither breakfast nor lunch, to the aforesaid bank, *rue* Scribe. The little man took my name, i.e. Wickwire, always a source of great difficulty for the French who haven't any 'w's in their language, and ran around trying to see if there was one like it written in a book somewhere...but no soap. I explained that you had sent the first *argent* in October and were planning to send more in November, right about now. He then got out a list of banks and pointed out that your bank (*la Banque royale*) does business with several Parisian banks but not this one. But you sent the money there, didn't you? I swore up and down that you did, anyway.

After this bit of fun and games I moped over to the métro feeling very glum, very, **very** hungry and wondering why-oh-why-did-I-come-here, etc. when I suddenly remembered the untouched backlog of $200.00 in traveller's cheques which, bless your hearts! You and Mum had given me. So, I'll be able to **eat**, hooray, between now and Dec. 5, the next bursary instalment day. Now I'm back in my room, having wolfed half-a-loaf of Hovis with honey, made myself a comforting cuppa tea and am writing to warn you that something is fishy in the banking world. Perhaps you can solve the *mystère* from the Halifax end? Poor Daddy, the only letters I address to you are about my financial troubles. Anyway, here is some more lighthearted fare with which to end the letter:

Colin Bergh, he of Amiens, turned up unexpectedly last Saturday afternoon. We went out to eat (Dutch treat as is customary here; besides I didn't know I'd be broke in two days) and then pottered around the streets. It was so good to see someone from home! We ended up in a *Dancing* place where we danced 'til we dropped. The French adore English words ending in '-ing' and here you see signs and labels that rock you back on your heels a bit, such as No Smoking,

Chewing-gum and Dancing; as well as sweater, pullover, tweed and (vital term) Water-closet, often shortened to WC and meaning 'toilet'. Also, to cook something *à l'anglaise* means, of course, to boil it to death (the French make endless, smug jokes about English cooking). What we call 'French leave' the French term *filer à l'anglaise*! And speaking of cooking, we had delicious chicken patty for lunch today. They do this from time to time so we won't filer à l'anglaise.

All my love, Nancy

Saturday, fin novembre

Dear Mamma:

Well! My new roommate has arrived. As you known, la Taciturne cleared out definitively about a week ago, leaving me her alcohol stove and an orange crate, so I was splendidly alone for a bit. Thursday evening a bunch of us went to the weekly film here at the Cité and then across the boulevard Jourdan for a hot chocolate. When I got home there was a sleeping form in the other bed so I tip-toed about, thinking to myself, 'Oh, help!' Friday morning the Somebody's alarm went off and we both sat up. It was still dark, being 7:00 AM, and I said to the shadowy figure across from me, "*Bonjour!*"

No answer.

Oh, dear. I clenched my fingers into the pillow and prepared myself for another silent *camarade de chambre*...but then she said very brightly, "*Bonjour!*" and we began to talk very easily about all sorts of things. Her name is Monique Artiguebieille (French girls are generally either Monique, Nicole, Andrée or Françoise) and her home is in Fontainebleau whither she returns for the weekends. She is a year younger than I and is doing a commercial course here. She has two older brothers and two younger ones, is very friendly and capable and chatty; we actually had breakfast together this morning in our room (something her predecessor never would have done). She had bread and coffee while I downed poached egg on biscotte and an orange. She says she simply couldn't eat orange or egg in the morning.

Monique struggles in English but wants to learn, which is good, because she will be more sympathetic about correcting my errors in French (we spoke halting English during breakfast). As you can see, even on such short acquaintance I know her much better and feel more at ease with her than with The Departed One. I've introduced her to Beth and Sarasu and Kaye Leslie, though doubtless she will want to chum with the French girls at the Franco-Brit. I only hope she and they don't band into a clique the way people of the same nationality tend to do. Oh well, even so, I expect my French to make big strides from now on. In fact, for once, I'm tired of speaking it as I've been ejecting French sentences all morning.

Last night M. and Mme Farmer, the directors of the Collège Franco-Britannique, *voulaient que nous assistions à une réception*[1] at nine o'clock, which everybody did. The basement room used for such things is long and narrow, with a floor tiled in multicoloured chips exactly like the lavatory floors and is painted an antiseptic green: the final decorator touch is that of burlap curtains of a dusty, rusty hue. Despite the surroundings, however, it managed to be quite pleasant. There was a little concert first, Franck's Sonata in something for Violin and Piano, played by two students (talented but not brilliant) and then Japanese dancing by a tiny, adorable Oriental girl to Japanese music and in costume. After the entertainment there was chaste dancing which ended promptly at midnight. Oh yes, white wine and ice-cream wafers as refreshment(!) Darn, we weren't told there'd be dancing. It really didn't matter except in the waltz numbers where, as I can't waltz very well, I blamed my clumsiness on the narrow skirt.

On yes! The movie I was seeing the night Monique arrived was a Russian silent film, supposed to be one of the landmarks in the history of film-making. It was called *le Cuirassé Potemkine*[2] and is about the Russian revolution, more particularly the naval part. It was superb. Also there was an animated Russian cartoon—very good—and a 'short' in colour featuring all the building and improvement going on in Moscow (pure propaganda of course). It seems that everything is pre-fabricated: walls, door-frames, slabs of concrete for sidewalks, etc.

so that an apartment can be build in less than five months. The films were in Russian but with French sub-titles.

Nicole Pouzargues, the French girl I told you about, has invited me to go to the cinéma with her and three of her friends tomorrow afternoon. I don't know what we are going to see but I'm excited and a teeny bit nervous about going with them. The friends speak no English, you see. In return I've invited her to come to the Cité next Tuesday evening when we're having a *soirée*, actually a St. Andrew's Night, complete with Scottish country dancing and refreshments.

And—O frabjous day! I received a notice from the bank this morning that my allowance has arrived, for which I am profoundly grateful. $ $ $ $ at last!

MONDAY EVENING

I'll finish this letter someday though it is taking rather a long time. To continue: Sunday morning, Sarasu and a very tall, red-headed Irish girl named Margaret Larminie, and I, went across Paris to the Methodist church. The service was held downstairs in the Ladies' Parlour because there is no heating in the church and the parlour boasts a propane gas heater. It was very comfy, somehow, despite the Dal. gym-type chairs. The church is having a Tea-and-Bake-Sale next Saturday afternoon which I intend to patronize.

I dashed from church to a lunch of—hold your nose! TRIPE with boiled potatoes soaked in tripe juice and, as a side dish, flabby, tasteless macaroni. Ugh! I couldn't eat it, double ugh! So I fled to my room and had cheese and bread and then went rattling into Paris on the métro to the cinéma. There I met Nicole and her three girlfriends, all French, all charming and with names that sounded faintly Gilbert and Sullivan: Paulette, Colette and Huguette. The first cinéma proved too expensive so we went to another which was showing *la Machine infernale* by Jean Cocteau, which is a modern and faintly shocking version of the Oedipus Rex story. Shocking in the sense that Sophocles' work was strictly tragic while Cocteau presents Jocasta as a rather dithery, frizzle-headed widow and includes scenes where soldiers speak in slang and so on. You feel that Cocteau is a brash upstart, taking such unpardonable liberties with such a great Greek tragedy but that is just why he did it—to shock us into realizing that, in real life, the characters may have acted exactly as he represents them. Do you remember—the first year I was at Dal.—how our *Cercle français* group was invited to Acadia to see a 'French' play? Well, the play was *la Machine infernale*, only in English translation.

After the film we all went into a *Salon de Thé* (and had coffee) and chatted. Paulette, Colette and Huguette asked me about Canada and I began to wax quite eloquent in probably atrocious French. At any rate they made me feel that I could talk to them which was exhilarating.

I got home just in time for dinner and, as I was late, there was nothing much left. Having about 150 francs in my pocket, I squandered 50 on a ham sandwich which you can buy in the canteen after the restaurant closes. Armed with this I was leaving the Maison internationale when Marc-Antoine suddenly materialized and asked if I wanted to go to the bal that evening at the Cuban House. Well, I was pretty tired but I thought, 'Well, why not?' so I precipitated myself upstairs and into a full skirt, wishing my hair were cleaner and gulping down the sandwich between zips.

The Maison Cuba was jam-packed full of people and music and smoke and Marc-Antoine, who claimed to have been studying all day, admitted to feeling rotten, so we left and had a coffee instead. He told me of a perfectly dreadful accident. A French-Canadian girl named Gisèle Froment was struck by a car as she was crossing the boulevard Jourdan and her skull was fractured. They operated twice in hopes of saving her but she is unconscious and dying. Her father has been sent for; I expect he's here by now. She was living in the Franco though I didn't know her. How awful!

Marc-Antoine also said that the larger proportion of fellows in the Maison canadienne are intellectual snobs of he worst kind and most unfriendly. Sprinkled among the snobs are a few *fils à papa*[3] plus a good fifteen homosexuals. Imagine! And I'm honour-bound to stick up for any and all Canadians here. Anyway, as Marc-Antoine said, this is all *laver le linge sale en famille.*[4] I am never to tell anyone who isn't Canadian.

I am writing this letter in bed, having slept all afternoon, only rousing myself for supper. I'm plain tuckered out! One doesn't realize—until one collapses—just how much extra energy it takes to do even minor things in Paris—and one is keyed to a high pitch, rushing here, rushing there. Anyway now I'm clean and relaxed, I've got some lovely money at last and no classes tomorrow.

Je vous embrasse tous trois, N.

P.S. I haven't found out how I'm getting to Grenoble yet but expect to leave about the 22nd of December. There is a direct train, Maria says.

[1] wished us to attend a reception
[2] The battleship Potemkin
[3] Daddy's boys
[4] washing the dirty laundry in private

December 1

From a letter to Duncan

.......I'm enclosing a piece from *Le Figaro* describing Mendès France's visit to Québec City: naturally it describes in detail the menu, so important to the French—and to students! We feel hungry all the time.

> ### LE DINER
> ### À Bois de Coulonges
>
> *Voici le menu du dîner offert en l'honneur du président du Conseil et de Mme Mendès France par M. Gaspard Fauteux, lieutenant-gouverneur de la province, à sa résidence de Bois-de-Coulonges : croustade fois gras Charvin; consommé diablotin; chevreuil forestier (de la propriété); pommes de terre noisette; petits pois;*

> *carottes Vichy; bombe glacée à l'érable; palmier; mignardises; café moka. Haut-Médoc, domaine de Serveau 1941; champagne Piper-Heidseck 1945; liqueurs.*
>
> Noted also : « *...c'est...la première fois qu'un président du Conseil visite Québec.* »
>
> LE FIGARO, 15 novembre, 1954 (A.F.P.)

Also (hope you're impressed!) Kaye Leslie and I saw *Faust* at the Paris Opéra last Friday evening. We are getting quite drunk on culture. Our seats, as usual, were just under the ceiling; I'll omit a detailed description of the tops of the singers' heads. But you know, I'd never been inside the Opéra before. Isn't it magnificent? The staircase with electric lights in the form of tapers, gosh, the building alone, *sans* performance, is enough for an evening's entertainment. Right above our heads were cupids and roses and hanging wreaths and, directly over our noses, a golden Venus posed her big toe. I felt as if I should be in a ball gown instead of a wool suit. Even though we were up there in the *poulailler*[1] we enjoyed the opera hugely, especially the peasant scenes, so alive and cheerful, like Breughel paintings come to life. At the end Marguerite (lovely voice) died on a pallet of straw with angel voices in the background, very moving.

[1] 'hen roost'

I do my Christmas shopping (But it's alcohol for my stone, not a wine bottle)

and sing Christmas carols

40

10 décembre, evening

Dear family:

Are you all in a good mood? Because I'm afraid I have some rather unfortunate news. Cousin Maria wrote me—her letter arrived this evening—saying that her noble Sicilian employers simply must begin employing her by the 22nd of December—don't ask me why—so she's leaving Grenoble and I shan't be able to go there for Christmas after all. Maria begged me not to tell you until after Christmas but I can't keep up a deception at all so I'm revealing the sorry news. What I will do is thus up in the air but even if I stay here there will be lots of company—Canadians especially—and I need never fear spending a dull holiday. But, in brackets, ISN'T THAT JUST LIKE MARIA?

Saturday I attended the Methodist church Tea-and-Bake-Sale with gusto and brought home a jar of lemon curd and a large white cake with lemony filling. That night I had a gastronomic party in my room consisting of guests Sarasu, Kaye Leslie and Jane Henry at which we ate cake and gossiped by the light of a candle (for atmosphere).

People are having love troubles all around me and I listen sympathetically to all. (I'm really very flattered that people want to tell me things in confidence.) I give them the benefit of my wisdom and experience, which consists in telling them exactly what they want to hear and not breaking in with personal anecdotes. At the same time I'm discovering a lot about myself. F'rinstance, I cannot control a sudden impulse to tears when something either quite disagreeable, or quite wonderful, happens. (Silly idiot!)

The St. Andrews soirée went off with éclat Tuesday evening. Thank goodness for my red plaid skirt! My guest Nicole Pouzargues seemed most impressed by the friendliness of les Britanniques.

Mucho love, Nancy

And here is Nancy, the hardy Canadian, enduring the relatively mild Parisian winter.

Tuesday, 14 déc.

Dear Folksies:

By the time you get this, Helen will be in the hospital minus a part of her interior. Do you suppose they'll let her keep the tonsils in a pickle jar?

I have a *petit* sore of the throat this morning myself but I don't think it's tonsils. We went Xmas carol singing on Sunday afternoon at Bicêtre hospital[1] and had to walk there—twenty minutes—in pouring rain. Then, yesterday, I added to the beastliness of the weather by forgetting my rubbers and daydreaming in the métro, so that I got off at Port-Royal instead of Luxembourg and had to walk the extra distance to the Sorbonne.

Our Bicêtre caroling went off very well, considering the depressing surroundings. The entire hospital looks like a collection of army barracks surrounding a Jane Eyre-style central building. Inside it was dismal, and dirty, and dark. Many of the patients were strapped into their beds. We carried a decorated Christmas tree with us from ward to ward and I felt utterly callous, striding in full of health and music and, after a token song or two, leaving the inmates to the gloom as we swept away, taking the evergreen symbol with us. There was a dance that evening at the Franco-Brit and Beth and I went, mainly to work off the bad effects of the hospital. Guess whom I met there? Ron Irving, a boy from Mount A. whom I remember from two years ago

A typical 'bal' at the Cité. Nancy and Beth circled.

when I toured with our silly one-actor, *Fantasy on an Empty Stage.* Remember? He was in the Mount Alison play, the one about Step-hen and the psychology—he played Step-hen. He's here studying art, thanks to the Navy, and is moving on to Rome soon.[2]

Did I tell you I saw *Cavalleria Rusticana* and *le Jongleur de Notre-Dame* at the Opéra Comique? *Cavalleria* was third-rate in my opinion. The chorus' singing was not quite ensemble, both heroes were fat and quite jammed into their Napoleonic tight pants and the heroine kept making the same gestures over and over again. I wish I could sic Leslie Pigot[3] on her—he'd soon change that. *Jongleur* was better, if very Roman Catholic. I'd heard, and now believe, that the Opéra Comique is not too, too good. But for the price, less than a dollar, who can complain?

The British Embassy is throwing a Christmas ball on December 20 at the Grand Hôtel and invitations have gone forth to all Britanniques and those from 'the colonies'. Swallowing the 'colonies' pill with difficulty I shall, nevertheless, attend. There will be a crowd going from here and though it's not formal, it will at least be a chance to dress up.

About Christmas: I have a 'sort-of' invitation which I haven't definitely accepted yet, to spend Christmas with a family connected with the Methodist Church. It's all being arranged through the minister and is very vague.

I mailed your Christmas presents ages ago and hope to heaven you get them! I've already received a package from Grandma which is tempting me from the top shelf.

Merry, Merry, Merry Christmas, Nancy

---

[1] Hospice de Bicêtre, founded 1633, rebuilt 1982.

[2] Ron Irving became Atlantic Regional Officer for the Canada Council and founded Theatre Prince Edward Island, remaining as artistic director until his retirement in 2004. He still acts (*Prospero*, a step up from *Step-hen!*).

[3] Leslie Pigot directed most of Dalhousie's Dramatic Society productions.

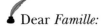

December 17

Dear Mom:

HALLELUJAH!

MERRY CHRISTMAS!

HAPPY EASTER!

HAPPY BIRTHDAY!

BE MY VALENTINE!

ETC. ETC.

Maria is staying in Grenoble

and

I am going there for Christmas!

H O O R A Y!

Her letter arrived today saying she's so happy she could cry. So am I. Now I've got to try and horn in on the *billet collectif*;[1] the last day for joining it is today, December 17. If not I'll go regular fare.

By the way, I've received no Christmas packages from you (except Grandma's). Funny! Haven't you got any of the magazines I've been mailing? Or my Christmas parcels?

Good night...all my love...sorry to have upset you even for a few days.

Nancy

[1] group ticket

December 21, evening

Dear *Famille:*

Christmas is so very near and I'm beginning to feel sentimental. Kaye Leslie (Kaye left for a trip to Germany on Saturday) has loaned me her radio and now it is playing a wonderful Bach chorale.

All my friends are leaving (thank goodness I am too) and I even feel rather soppy about it. Imagine what a blubbery session there'll be in June when we have to separate for good! Beth goes tomorrow evening, Sarasu on Thursday afternoon. Jane Henry has already gone. Monique leaves for Fontainebleau tomorrow and most of the fellows from the Franco-Brit have trooped off already. And we're all so happy to be going somewhere for a traditional Christmas with all the old customs. It seems that a nice, Yule-y fireplace and a tree surrounded by relatives have an irresistible appeal, even to the most enfranchised and bohemian of students.

Isn't it funny how one can be brave and independent all year and then crumple into a wad of sentiment at Christmas-time?

Last night I went to the British Embassy's dance at the Grand Hôtel. It was marvellous. I went with a Welsh lad named Rhys, wore my festive purple rig and reeked of *Moment Suprême* perfume which I broke down and finally bought with part of Daddy's Christmas money. The Grand Hôtel is immense and the ballroom has a ceiling as high as a theatre, elegantly curved. From it there drips a gorgeous crystal chandelier from which was hung an enormous bunch of fresh mistletoe. Sir Gladwyn Jebb, the ambassador, made a nice little speech and we all danced and threw coloured streamers and confetti. I waltzed and whirled until my shoes seemed almost worn out. There were rumbas and sambas and polkas—it was marvellous and we didn't get home until after 2:00 AM.

THE
"BRITISH COLONY COMMITEE"
INVITE YOU TO A:
CHRISTMAS DANCE
MONDAY 20TH DECEMBER 1954
AT THE
GRAND HOTEL
ENTRANCE : BOULEVARD DES CAPUCINES, PARIS
DANCING FROM 8.30 PM TO 1.00 AM
FLOOR SHOW
Informal dress
there is no admission charge but an opportunity
will be given to contribute to expense.

The night before that, Marc-Antoine and I went to a real little *boîte* of a night-club, tiny and pokey and dark, with a creaky, lumpy floor and a be-bop orchestra and jitterbugging Africans with French girls in tight slacks. We drank *vin rosé* and danced and afterwards tramped up and down the boul' Mich', finally settling in on a midnight *restaurateur* with an order for *krapfens* (a sort of doughnut) and coffee. We took a taxi home as it was 3:00 AM (no métro) and the chauffeur nearly scared the liver out of me, he drove so fast, while swearing, in approved fashion, at all the other taxi drivers we nearly ran into.

The night before THAT...I went to bed.

Mrs. Coffin[1] wrote me a Christmas note saying that her son Tommy had asked 'what Nancy was doing in Paris?' At that very moment Nancy was tearing out her hair, having sent a *pneumatique*,[2] a phone call and left a personal note with the fellow who was organizing the billet collectif—and having received no answer. I would have said to Tommy that, as for Paris, Nancy was spending her time trying to buy a ticket to get out of it! Eventually the collective ticket chap phoned and said everything was OK and that he'd send someone out to collect my money and give me my ticket, all of which he did, bless his little French heart. I was so frantic by then (this all took place this morning) wondering how I'd ever get to Grenoble that I burst into a flood of happy tears on the phone. I tell you, there's never a dull moment around this place.

I leave at ten tomorrow eve from the Gare de Lyon and arrive in Grenoble the next morning at seven. For Christmas I've bought Maria a bottle of *parfum* and a box of chocolates. Hope my *bonne humeur* survives sitting up all night!

Your Xmas package hasn't come yet, which is rather a pity but typical of French postal service so I'm not awfully surprised. Perhaps it will arrive dramatically in the last mail tomorrow and I can bear it triumphantly to Grenoble like one of the *Rois mages*.[3]

Dec. 22

I'm all packed—it's raining out—going to dinner tonight with Ron Irving who's seeing me off—your package didn't come but there's a mail strike at Gare St. Lazare so it's probably held up there—I asked that it be sent on to Grenoble if it comes—oodles of love,

Nancy

---

[1] The Coffins were Halifax neighbours.
[2] in Paris: letter in a pneumatic tube, forwarded via an underground compressed air system.
[3] the Three Kings

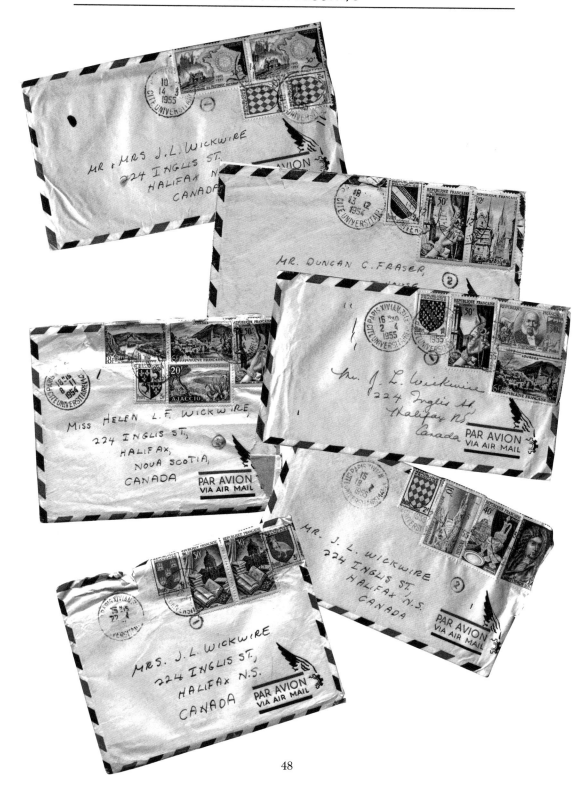

ECLAIRAGE

(the light goes on)

January 3 to April 2, 1955

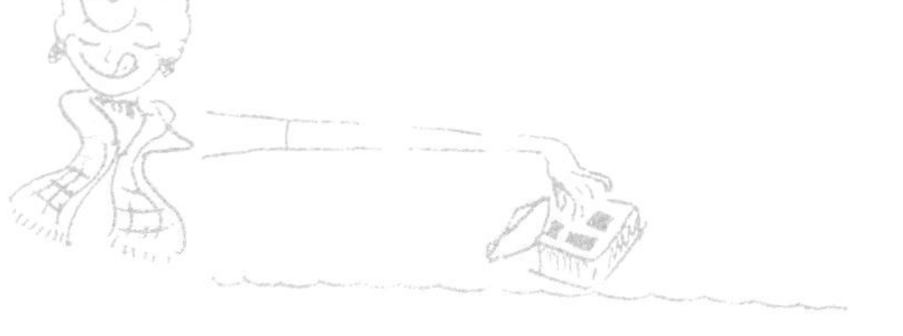

From BRITANNICA BOOK OF THE YEAR, 1955

JANUARY

January 3: U.S. state dept. declared 27% of the area of the U.S. off limits to Soviet citizens.

January 4: Japanese government announced that the U.S. had agreed to pay $200,000 compensation for the damage and injury to Japanese fishermen after the Bikini hydrogen bomb explosion in 1954.

January 19: Pres. Eisenhower's press conference was filmed for television and news reels for the first time.

January 25: Soviet government formally terminated the state of war between the U.S.S.R. and Germany.

FEBRUARY

February 1: Princess Margaret, sister of Queen Elizabeth II of the United Kingdom, arrived at Port of Spain, Trinidad, for a month's tour of the British West Indies.

February 3: Prague radio announced that Czechoslovakia had ended the state of war with Germany.

February 10: British house of commons rejected, by vote of 245 to 214, a motion for the suspension of the death penalty for a five-year trial period.

February 23: French national assembly voted, 369 to 210, to confirm Radical leader Edgar Faure as premier.

February 27: West German bundestag approved the Paris agreements providing, among other things, for the termination of allied occupation and the admission of western Germany to NATO and the projected western European union.

MARCH

March 30: Motion picture On the Waterfront received the Academy of Motion Picture Arts and Sciences as the best picture of 1954; awards for best starring performances went to Marlon Brando and Grace Kelly.

The letter mailed from Grenoble with a description of the all-night train ride and my introduction to that city (Maria met me on a bicycle!) did not arrive. A partial description of the Christmas Day celebrations at the Bouglé household (where Maria was boarding) was, thank goodness, preserved in a letter posted from Paris to Duncan.

January 3, 1955

From a letter to Duncan

. . .here I am, back in my room at the good old Cité after a super-terrific time in Grenoble with Maria. She lives in a *pension de famille*[1] (M. et Mme Bouglé) and I stayed there with her. The three children of the family were bright and chatty and we were soon *tu-toi-ing*[2] each other; and I picked up a handy number of filthy expressions and naughty songs.

Beside Maria and myself and the five Bouglés there was another *pensionnaire*, Maureen, (an English girl) and two New York girlfriends of Maria's, Barbara and Betty, who'd been touring France and 'dropped in' for a visit. All these people crammed into the second floor flat of an old house! We were three to a bed and twenty arms around the table. Besides this, Maria's and Maureen's student friends kept popping in so that the flat was never quiet. Maria, who has the biggest bedroom, had installed a Christmas tree in it. Everyone comes in to admire it—it's the first one they've ever had in the house. Speaking of beds, Maria has two single beds side by side, cunningly made up with single sheets and blankets which overlap at mid-point in order to accommodate three bodies. Betty (who is, um, plump) and Maria and I sleep in it. But there's a problem. She who is in the middle finds herself stark uncovered if the two outside ones decide to roll over! So we rotate sleeping positions: left, right and centre. There's no heating in the flat, you see, except a stove in the dining room.

On Christmas Eve everybody went to *la Messe de minuit.* There were two Masses, one after the other—I might have gone to sleep right there but for an interesting diversion—a girl fell into the confession box because the door hadn't been latched properly and she leaned on it. After Mass, Madame Bouglé served us a *réveillon*[3] which went on and on, aided by wine and song, until the wee, wee *heures*. Christmas day we had turkey with the feathered, beaked head still on it in proper French style; and three kinds of wine. I got rather tipsy (along with everyone else), sang, 'While strolling through the park one day' complete with gestures, and the afternoon saw us all asleep in our beds.

Love, N.

[1] boarding house
[2] *Tu* (thou) and *toi* (thee) are acceptable when addressing an intimate, child, servant or animal, otherwise *vous* (you) is obligatory in both singular and plural.
[3] Christmas Eve feast

January 2, 1955
Collège Franco-Britannique

Dear Family:

The silence in my room is quite eerie after eleven days of constant hullabaloo. Never mind, I need the peace and quiet, though it is sad to leave Maria and the Bouglé family and all the friends I made in Grenoble.

I hope you got my Christmas epistle, posted from Grenoble? As you can tell, I had a perfectly super time. It got better and better as we went rolling and singing along towards New Year's.

PART ONE

After Christmas Maria, plus Barbara-and-Betty from New York, plus Maureen-from-England, plus Thierry, the Bouglés' 17-year-old son (on Xmas leave from his *service militaire*), plus Séneschal, Maria's student admirer—and I— went skiing for two days in succession on the most beautiful mountain ever created, Chamrousse. It was high up above the clouds and covered in pure, white snow. Below us in the valley where Grenoble lies we could see a sea of cottony mist but on the mountain everything was cold and sparkling, yet warm with winter sun.

We'd all of us spent two days beforehand tagging around after Maria, who was trying to rent us skis and poles and boots. Her boyfriend Séneschal is, as she herself says, typically French, i.e. he was absolutely no help. Having presented himself as the expert he'd accompany us half-way to somewhere and then, getting his precious dander up at some little thing, take off and sulk. All this had no effect on Maria except to amuse her. She plodded on and somehow we all got skis and poles and boots and socks and warm sweaters.

First day, Dec. 29: Up at 6:30 in the pitch dark, we hopped on a special bus full of skiers and rattled up to Chamrousse, passing old stone farmhouses which clung to the steep edges of the alp.

As we climbed, the hoar frost turned to snow and suddenly the sun appeared, lighting up the world with a thousand twinkles and outlining the evergreens with their robes of white. Finally we rolled up to an enormous wooden ski lodge, above which were the slopes. The sky was a clear, sweet blue, almost navy in contrast to the snow in places.

First, we had cups of hot coffee in one of the many small restaurants which line the ground floor of the lodge. Maria and Thierry and Séneschal knew how to ski, supposedly, so they took off with a flourish while Maureen and I struggled philosophically with our ski fixtures, humming little tunes to ourselves. Barbara-and-Betty stayed in the restaurant.

Maureen and I spent most of the morning going up a ten-foot slope in order to reach a place whence we could ski (and fall) down again. It was pretty icy where the sun hadn't yet shone and we struggled along, smacking our skis into the snow sideways and vowing to learn how to ski properly if we never did anything else. After the lunch which Madame Bouglé packed for us, we felt game for another try. The lunch was a moose-choker but delicious: huge slabs of ham between thick slices of French bread, plus jam likewise, dozens of hard-boiled eggs, cheese and oranges.

The afternoon was much more successful as I'd finished explaining by that time how it was that I was Canadian and didn't know how to ski. I even said that my sister jumped on my skis when I was twelve and broke them, which of course is no excuse.

The sun had softened the snow by now and Maureen and I were gliding down small slopes with considerable ease, when someone decided that it would be a good idea to take the *téléski* to the top of the hill where there were stretches of gentle inclines. The téléski is a forbidding machine consisting of an endless, moving sort of clothesline on which hang staves with round discs at the bottom ends. You hang onto the stave, put your legs around the disc and hope for the best. I found myself going rapidly uphill on my derrière. If this was a hoot, the *pièce de résistance* was getting off the thing at the top without sliding all the way back down the hill. The only way I could manage it was to let go the stave, fall to my hands and knees like an infant and grovel helplessly. (By the next day, though, I'd got quite expert at the téléski.)

Hereupon I completely revised my opinion of Séneschal who turned out to be a perfect lamb as he spent all afternoon with Maureen and myself, trying to show us how to turn without falling.

The mountain is at its most beautiful about 5:00 PM when the sky begins to get winter pink and the snow suddenly puts forth blue shadows; and the long, lithe silhouettes of skiers begin the final jaunt down the slope to the waiting busses. And what a glorious feeling, the wind in your face and hair as you successfully descend a long snow slope!

Casualties: Thierry dislocated his knee and Maria had a bump on hers as big as an egg. Betty and Barbara didn't ski at all: Maureen and I had fallen down the oftenest but I'll bet we had the most fun.

Second day, Dec. 30: At 6:30 AM I decided, wrenching open my eyes and experimenting with a pair of legs stiff from skiing all night in bed, that human beings must be idiots to strap a couple of boards to their feet and then see how far they can slide down a hill in 59.1 seconds: however, we hoisted our gear upon our shoulders and boarded the bus.

The second day Chamrousse was even more beautiful. I was so stiff that I took more photos than I skied: Maureen and I mostly pottered about on easy runs.

PART TWO

The following day everyone was *courbaturé*[1] but happy and lo! It was New Year's Eve. Maria, Maureen, Betty, Barbara and I got dressed up and set off with Thierry and Séneschal to a party at the students' hangout, called CUIG. Here we had champagne and pastries and dancing. By 2:30 AM everyone was tired, especially after skiing, so we decided to go to the Trois Dauphins to dance some more. The Trois Dauphins is a pretty ritzy hotel and the orchestra was tops. Unfortunately we couldn't stay without paying (Séneschal had thought that by that hour we could get in free). To compensate, we ducked into an all-night restaurant and had raviolis and some pretty strong wine; got home about 4:30, dropped into bed and slept until noon.

For the New Year's *déjeuner* we had rabbit, which I'd never tasted before but which I liked, and a lovely bakery cake, French-frosted (no-one ever thinks of home-baking a cake in France). That afternoon Thierry, who considers himself a *séducteur* even though he's only seventeen, invited me out for a walk. We boarded the *téléphérique* which swoops you across the river Isère to the top of a hill overlooking Grenoble. Here the romantic remains of an old fort, La Bastille, awaited us. The Bastille had a *Thé dansant* so Thierry bought us two filters[2] and we danced a bit, Thierry whispering reassuringly in my ear that he was *experimenté*,[3] having been initiated by an 'older woman', all of which alarmed me.

And after supper we all went to the cinéma; and the next day I left.

PART THREE

I paid Madame Bouglé $20.00 even for eleven days' room and board, kissed her goodbye and gave her a little box of chocolates as a parting gift. Maria, Maureen, Thierry and Séneschal accompanied me and my suitcase to the train station—old M. Bouglé drove us there, all six of us jammed into his antiquated tin lizzie and all giggling like idiots. It was an evening departure; the train station is pretty small; yet I couldn't find the *billet collectif* group. 'Well,' I thought, 'maybe they're all aboard already.' So I hopped on the train and was sent off to Maria's prankish shouts of, "Don't forget to wash your underwear!" which fortunately no one around me could understand. I settled down with seven others in a 3rd class compartment next to an old lady in black who kept muttering, "*Courants d'air!*"[4]

Maria and Nancy in Grenoble. Behind us is Mme B.

About 5:00 AM, as we neared Paris, the *contrôleur*[5] came in for the tickets. Big fuss. My *billet collectif* had expired the day before, according to him. Fortunately a young man in our compartment was in the same boat which at least gave me moral support. A first-rate argument ensued; from what I could understand of his rapid French, the contrôleur seemed to be accusing us of trying to defraud the S.N.C.F. But the Gare de Lyon was packed with people and we looked so despairing that he finally shrugged and let us through. With Haligonian sang-froid I hoisted my suitcase onto the métro and rode back to the Cité in the cold dawn.

There, a-waiting, were piles and piles of letters and cards and a beautiful pair of earrings and pin to match from Duncan. (Still no Christmas box from you!)

Sour note. I've only had one monthly period since I came and that was in October. It worries me a bit so I'm going to see the Cité universitaire doctor on Wednesday. I expect it's the change in living and the excitement; anyway, 'curse' or no 'curse', I'd rather have it than not. Being a boursière the visit won't cost me anything.

In this minor key I remain, Yours truly, etc.

[1] stiff   [2] filtered coffee—very strong

[3] sexually experienced   [4] "There's a draft!"   [5] conductor

5 janvier

Dear Mamma:

We had a snowfall yesterday and there's still a bit left though it looks most forlorn. Winter here is a very distant cousin of our Canadian variety.

Well, I went to the doctor this morning and he examined me, took my blood pressure and prescribed a shot a day of something for four days running after which all should be hunky-dory. I'm going over to get the first injection before lunch. He says there's nothing physically wrong, just the change of climate and food and the excitement. He was awfully nice and made me feel at ease, even in only a bra and panties. I went down the boulevard Jourdan afterwards to get the prescribed *médicament*[1] from the *pharmacien*[2] and on the way stocked up on fruit, cold cream, film and bought myself a pretty potted hyacinth for a dollar. All the florists' shops display daffodils and tiny, white jonquils, tulips, hyacinths and violets. It is like a dream, looking in their windows.

You should see the displays of the *charcuterie*[3] and *poissonerie*[3] shops here. They put their wares, already prepared, in the window. I've seen turkeys and pheasants, all cooked, with the wings, head and tail stuck on afterwards (feathers and all) as ornament. Also, whole, split pigs decorated with roses and chrysanthemums, with a long ribbon of tomato-coloured paste down the side, rosettes of something else adorning it; and of course, the original fish head and tail for that final, gracious touch.

The French put a lot of emphasis on the Visual Effect. Their pastry is always elaborately decorated. Chocolate boxes abound with ribbons, lace and artificial flowers and even the women are judged on looks alone.

News: Kaye Leslie is leaving for Canada on the 15th of January and is docking in Halifax, before she takes the boat train to Lévis. I'll find out what day she arrives and have a favour to ask you: could you meet her and (if she has time) take her home for a cup of tea and, if not, see that she gets safely on the train? She has a job with the newspaper *Le Soleil* in Québec and that is why she is going home at such a wild time of year.

I must tell you about the extravagant love letter I received yesterday from Thierry. I was really very touched—it is a masterpiece of prose, suitable for framing and typically French—that is, typical of the melancholy, serious, self-centred French adolescent: in short, romantic, in the 19th century tradition. In it he says that I have been an example to him, he wants to live like me, I am the ideal young woman, etc. etc.

Poor Thierry! Still, I must admit, it's flattering to have worshippers from afar, as long as they stay AFAR.

Love, La Belle Dame Sans Merci.

[1] medicine
[2] druggist
[3] pork and delicatessen shop *and* fish shop

January 11

Dear Mither:

Isn't 8:30 an ungodly hour to begin classes? If these *Histoire de l'art* lectures weren't so good, I'd never make it. There are compensations—among them, watching the sky get lighter each morning as the days lengthen. In springtime I expect the early mornings will be quite poetic. As yet, *il fait nuit*[1] until nearly 9:00 AM. Paris is one hour ahead of Greenwich Time, you see.

Last night Margaret Larminie (Irish), Elizabeth Wade (English) and I went out to dinner as a treat. Elizabeth knew of a restaurant not far from the Luxembourg métro stop to which her papa had taken her more than once.

The restaurant overlooks the Luxembourg gardens and is called the Médicis, doubtless because the Luxembourg gardens and palace were built for Marie de Médicis, one of the Italian Queens of France. We were the only non-French speakers and the sole women in the Médicis, which seemed to be full of *hommes d'affaires* taking their business colleagues out to dine. Chattering and laughing girlishly in English we were thus a double curiosity. It was a lovely meal and afterwards we went to a small cinéma which was showing *Le désert vivant*[2] by Walt Disney and which I'd been dying to see for months. The commentary was in

Near the Luxembourg métro stop—the Panthéon in the background. The Panthéon closely resembles the venerable Sorbonne.

French and—joy of joys! I understood THE WHOLE THING. There was a French 'short' before the feature film, a clever parody of *les Trois Mousquetaires* wherein Cardinal Richelieu tripped all over the place in his haste to outsmart D'Artagnan and the impossibly foppish Duke of Buckingham. The Cardinal, by the way, is one of the most revered figures in the history of the University of Paris.

This afternoon I'd just finished off a letter to 'Cher Professeur Chavy' when Margaret knocked on the door and asked me if I'd like to sample the Christmas cake she'd brought back from Ireland with her. Would I? I went up to her room (which is directly above mine) where she made coffee and sliced up a delicious, dark fruit cake, trimmed with almond paste. The English (and Irish) make such rich fruit cake! I had two wedges, nevertheless, with black coffee, and felt surfeited for hours.

Monique and I are taking over the rental of Kaye Leslie's radio from the 15th of January. It's only 660 francs a month which, divided between us, makes less than a dollar each.

Perhaps feeling that a French person born will triumph where a foreigner fails, Monique smuggled in a small, electric cooking element from home and we tried it Monday morning. Pouf! went all the lights. Our darned wiring just won't take the extra charge, though electric elements work beautifully across the hall. The reason may be (it has been suggested) that the system of wiring is vertical, from cellar to roof, and we have the kitchen under us absorbing all the voltage and wattage (I don't really understand electricity). Well, perhaps. Anyway, that made the third time I've had to report to the concierge that the lights won't march. He didn't seem perturbed. Perhaps it's a common occurrence?

I can hear the birds enjoying the rain. The other day a poor, little feathered fellow flew in my open window by mistake. He was soft grey and yellow and scared to death; and it didn't take him a minute to get out again.

I have booked a tentative passage home on the Samaria leaving Le Havre on July 1 but since my final bursary payment isn't due until July 5, I don't know...maybe they'll give it to me a few days earlier? I don't want to stay here after June 30 because summer rents are double the price and you risk getting kicked out anyway (Dorothy Yates was last year). Besides, if I'm to teach next year, I must enroll in the Dal. summer course.

Now, if you'll excuse me, I must go and shrink my pyjamas. Tuesday is laundry day for me.

X X X O O O, Nancy

[1] It's dark
[2] *The Living Desert*

15 janvier

Dear Papa:

Your letter saying everything was fine about Kaye Leslie [1] arrived this morning, like the hero on his white horse, to save the maiden at the last minute. Kaye is leaving this very afternoon.

Beth, Monique and I took her to a funny little French (naturally) restaurant near here for a farewell luncheon. Everything is meticulously ready for *le départ*. Kaye isn't like Dorothy Yates who was still packing frantically an hour before her train left for the south of

France. She is wearing her new grey suit, incredibly chic, bought on the Champs Elysées, has had her hair done and is looking altogether very smart. She's left me her radio, which is playing sweet strains into my right ear, a tube of condensed milk, half-a-box of sugar, half-a-jar of mustard, some spot remover and the address of her coiffeur; so altogether I didn't do too badly.

SOCIETY PAGE

Kaye and I, dressed to the teeth, went to a cocktail party last Wednesday eve *chez* M. Désy, the Canadian ambassador. *Chez* turned out to be an ivory and gold palace in the ritziest district, with gloved servants and carpeted parlours. Very chez indeed! We were introduced to M. and Mme Désy and then set loose to circulate. We circulated right towards the hors d'oeuvres which were delicious. I

L'Ambassadeur du Canada et Madame Jean DESY vous prient de venir à une réception qui aura lieu à leur résidence, 135 rue du Faubourg Saint-Honoré, le mercredi 12 janvier 1955, de 17 à 19 heures.

ate so many that I hadn't room for any supper. One could easily tell which of the guests were students as we formed a solid line around the food.

After the cocktails, I met a couple of German classmates at the Théâtre Montparnasse-Gaston Baty, where we saw *l'Alouette*[2] by Jean Anouilh, the modern playwright. All the critics say it's brilliant. At this stage I applaud anything I can understand and, yippee! I hardly missed a word.

Last night Monique and I headed off to the Théâtre National Populaire (or TNP), to see *Macbeth*, in French. Wisely the French troupe didn't try to imitate a British production but did it their own way, i.e. extremely stylized. The TNP favours a minimal décor; their black backdrops set off brilliant costumes which, for *Macbeth*, were in solid colours of scarlet, yellow and turquoise. This sort of thing suits French romantic tragedies such as *Ruy Blas*,[3] (the first TNP production I saw) but...hmmmm...the jury is out on *Macbeth*.

Tonight (never a dull moment) there's a reception at the Maison internationale just for us, *les professeurs de français à l'étranger*[4] and, on the 15th, the Scots at the Franco-Brit are cutting the haggis and serenading Bobby Burns. Och, I'll be a r-r-eal Scot when I r-r-etur-r-rn!

The day Kaye arrives in Halifax (next Sunday) Nancy will be trotting out to the Musée de l'Homme, an anthropological museum dedicated to the different races of mankind. I happened to meet a real anthropologist at the Ambassador's party and he is going to show me through. I've been planning to go for ages and now I shall have an expert as guide.

We have had the room of our *phonétique* class changed seven times so far and the latest move has landed us in the Maison de la Mutualité, a huge, modern edifice. The other evening during our lesson, the big assembly hall next door was full of men, smoking and muttering, while another addressed them in strident tones from the platform. As the session drew to a close the noise rose to a crescendo; shouts, curses, chairs banging, etc. It was, I found out, a meeting of Paris' taxi-drivers, protesting against the new ruling that they must put a sign saying TAXI on top of their cabs, with a light inside for the nighttime!

I've learned several 'everyday' French expressions which I hereby offer you in case you'd like to add some polish to your conversation. In order of increasing irritation, they are: *Zut!* (Heck!), *Flûte!* (Rats!) and *Merde!* (Shit!) The last is my favourite, of course.

Oh, and could you send me a couple of facecloths? The French ones I find next to useless (*Zut!*) as they're made in the form of a mitt and fall apart in no time.

As I write, the radio is crooning, of all things, 'Seven lonely days I cried and cried for you'. It sounds better in French.

Nancy

---

[1] Kaye's Sorbonne studies got her jobs at *Le Soleil*, then two Toronto magazines. In 1958 she married Graham Thistle and accompanied him on his European postings with the Department of National Defence. The Thistles retired to Manotick, Ontario.

[2] Joan of Arc is the *alouette* (lark). Anouilh's play opened in 1953.

[3] Victor Hugo's poetic drama, set in the decadent Spain of 1698.

[4] 'French teachers abroad'

Dearest Mamma:

You deserve a whole row of bright pink medals and a mink coat.

Yum, yum, yum!

One of the Christmas cake and cookie packages arrived last evening.

Thank you, *merci, gracias*!

I took two pieces of cake and some (unbroken) cookies over to two of my friends in the Maison canadienne, Marc-Antoine and John Clark, then had a party in my room for Sarasu, Elizabeth Wade and Monique. All pronounced the sweets **delicious**. Where there's life, there's hope, even when the French postal system intervenes.

I seem to be doing all sorts of things this month. Sunday morning there's a *visite* to the Luxembourg palace which has been arranged through the Maison canadienne. 'Tis where the French Senate sits and can only be viewed by special appointment. Sunday evening, **if** the Seine doesn't overflow (it's abnormally high), Jane Henry and I are going to see *la Cerisaie*, a translation of Tchekhov's *The Cherry Orchard*, which everyone says is very good; it has been playing here for years.

The Luxembourg visit, by the way, was announced at a meeting of all Canadian students at the Maison canadienne the other evening. Proceedings were conducted mainly in French-Canadian French. I can distinguish between different French accents now and find Canadian French quite unlike the Parisian variety. The Parisians look down on it, of course.

We recently had several days of spring-like sunshine and so, my spirits keyed up, I courageously entered a *chemisier*[1] shop and demanded a blue-and-white striped cotton blouse. It has long sleeves and turned-back French cuffs and a pointy collar—like a man's shirt. Also, I bought one of those sexy, long ropes of mashed pearls and gold which you wind a hundred times around your neck, tra-la. Also a red leather belt to match my shoes. I feel quite swish in these things tho' I still can't match Parisian chic.

Beth Ogilvie has her third *grippe* of the season and is in bed with it. I haven't had a cold yet—miraculous thing. Perhaps it's all the fruit I eat? I've lost weight, too, though not much (do **not** worry). For mental health, I've got a Van Gogh landscape and a bright red Dufy violin pinned above my bed.

Maria writes from Grenoble that she has nearly finished her academic papers for the Adelphi School and will be able to move on, finally, to Sicily. She also says that Thierry has been suspended from military school for bullying new arrivals. Ha! Perhaps they'll hire him at the Comité d'Accueil (remember my first day in Paris?)

Do you know I haven't had a tub bath in three and a half months? I'm so used to showers now that I almost prefer them, even though they're cold.

Muchissimo love, Nancy

P.S. I have just finished reading *1984* by George Orwell. It is perfectly terrifying—but I couldn't put it down.

[1] shirt-maker

Tuesday afternoon, January 25
Dear Parents:

Please don't fret about the strayed Christmas presents. I did get one parcel already so there's hope the others will turn up. Nevertheless, when I take this over to the Post Office to mail, I shall **demand** a postal search and I shan't take a Gallic shrug of the shoulders for an answer.

Last Sunday afternoon I was getting ready to go to the Musée de l'Homme with Monsieur Renaud (remember? the Canadian anthropologist?) when my buzzer rang. I ran down half-dressed to discover it wasn't he at all but Nouhé, asking me to the Indo-Chinese New Year's ball the following night. Well, it was rather a last-minute invitation but Jane Henry was going—and I was dying to put on my long formal for once—so I accepted.

The punctual M. Renaud arrived on the dot of two o'clock and we had a very scientific afternoon. The Musée has heaps of skulls, normal and deformed; about seven human foetus (foeti? fetuses?) pickled, in different stages of growth; shrunken heads, apes' skeletons and a huge section on primitive art, African war masks, drums and so on. We weren't nearly finished when the bell rang, forcing us to leave. After that, we walked down to the Pont de l'Alma to see the famous Zouave, which is Paris' register for the height of the Seine. The Zouave is the stone figure of an African soldier in baggy breeches, with bare chest and a tiny, pointed beard. The water usually just bathes his feet but yesterday it swirled above his belt. All of Paris had come to look at him despite the greyness of the day—I could barely see the feet of the Eiffel tower while the top was hidden in thick mist.

M. Renaud then suggested that we have dinner in town, to which I was readily agreeable since Sunday meals at the Maison internationale are truly abominable. We finally hit upon a small *boîte* across from a theatre. Theatre people with orange faces and false eyelashes kept piling in and out, grabbing a snack between the matinée and evening performances. I had a tomato salad and

The Zouave in April 2001—water to his knees. In 1955 the Seine reached his waist.

we both had chicken with *petits pois*[1] and goat's cheese to finish off with.

I had to rush home because that evening I was going with Jane to see *la Cerisaie*. I dashed in, cut off a piece of my wonderful cake to give to M. Renaud as a thank-you (also because he'd not been able to take any dessert at the restaurant since I was in a rush), collected Jane and off we went.

The Cherry Orchard is the story of a noble Russian family before the Revolution. Though nearly penniless they refuse, sentimentally, their one chance for survival—sell the old cherry orchard for building lots. Their creditors seize the estate and, as the play draws to a close, we hear the chop! chop! of the axes, cutting down the cherry trees. It was funny, poignant and pathetic at the same time.

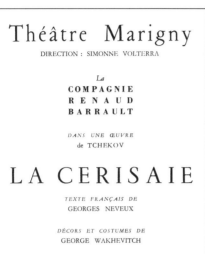

Madeleine Renaud   Jean-Louis Barrault

When we got home, we talked about what we would wear tomorrow night. Jane has a ballet-length gown of navy blue organdie embroidered in white, with a strapless top and little red shoes, while I was planning to wear my (equally strapless) floor-sweeping turquoise net over taffeta, having ascertained beforehand that we would be picked up in a taxi.

Alors, to bed. *Mais*, at 6 AM the next morning…I had the most awful pains in my tummy and a fearful headache! Monique helped me take a couple of aspirins before she left for school and I went back to sleep for a while but the spasms stayed all day. It was horrible. At times I felt like vomiting but nothing would come up. Monique came back in the afternoon and found me crying like a little girl. I felt so sort of weak and hurt-y and all I wanted was Mamma to come and sit beside me and tell me stories to make me laugh. But Monique is a dear and she understood—ruffled my hair, begged me not to cry and got me some water for another aspirin. We decided that I had food poisoning from something I'd eaten the evening before.

Anyway, Cinderella couldn't go to the ball. I missed all my classes and am missing them today as well! And I'm still weeping.

By this evening, though, I expect to rally because, at 9:00 PM precisely, I'll have the rare and wonderful opportunity of seeing, nay, even tasting, a haggis. Imagine coming to Paris to meet a haggis! My digestion should be able to handle it as I'm told it's mostly oatmeal. You don't eat the actual sheep's stomach, mercifully, as the mixture is only cooked in it and then spooned out like dressing out of a turkey.

I've just finished reading *Jane Eyre* and as usual after letting myself get right into a book, the author's style rings in my head for days. If only French literary style could be absorbed so easily!

Speaking of French style, I'm going to give you another list of helpful French expressions which I use dozens of times every day. The French are great on little verbal niceties which **must** be uttered, usually on parting, thus proving that the speaker has been well brought-up. They are: *Au revoir!* (See you around!); *A bientôt!* (See you shortly!); *A tout à l'heure!* (See you within the hour!) and *Bonsoir!* (Good night!). *Bonne nuit,* by the way, has a rather scandalous connotation so is rarely said; and finally, *Pardon!* (Get out of my way, you oaf!) *Pardon!* is such a useful word. One can shove oneself ahead in a queue, say, '*Pardon!*' and get away with it.

Do put out an extra blob of peanut butter for the chickadees for me. Actually you might send me some peanut butter—they've never heard of it in France—also a small package of maple sugar which is another thing they've never tasted.

I'm about to begin reading an erotic novel, *Sons and Lovers,* by D.H. Lawrence. My Oxford-educated friends say it's one of the best in modern fiction. Compared to the British girls here I have a lot of literary catching-up to do! Then I solemnly vow to switch exclusively to novels in French.

The End, with love, N.B.W.

[1] green peas (tinned)

Dear Family:

Guess what is melting on my tongue right now?

A piece of Daddy's home-made chocolate fudge!

And what I'm wearing on my ears?

A pair of Nova Scotia crest earrings!

And what I'm going to put around my neck this morning?

A Nova Scotia tartan scarf!

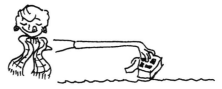

Your missing Christmas parcel has arrived. (Excuse me while I have another bite.) What fun and what a mess! Wrapping paper everywhere. Thank you for everything, especially the tea cosy. My pot now looks so handsome, I'm tempted to display it as an ornament. As for the fudge, I ate three pieces just while opening my Christmas stocking. Monique screamed with laughter when she saw the shower cap (another North American oddity, it seems). Thank you a zillion times.

So, now, the only parcel still at large is the one with the second fruit cake. I have high hopes of its arriving next Thursday as both other boxes came on Thursdays, exactly one week apart.

Monique and I went last night to the weekly film here at the Cité. It was a tortured thing called *le Journal d'un Curé de campagne,* from a novel by Georges Bernanos. The hero is a young priest of very delicate health who is disliked by his parishioners but keeps going doggedly on until he kills himself with neglect and overwork. Br-r-r.

This Saturday evening, Birgitta Ekman, a Swedish-Canadian girl from Alberta whom I met at the Ambassador's party, has invited me to a variety concert, called a *music-hall* in French. I am told that Parisians themselves flock to these music-halls so it should be fun.

HAGGIS REPORT

Och, aye, I made it to the Bobby Burns supper, with haggis

and turnips and tatties and a'. The haggis was very spicy and came (big disappointment) out of a can. Several Scots read verses they'd composed for toasts and addresses to the haggis, etc., all in Scots dialect and pretty clever, too. Afterwards a troupe of Breton dancers gave us a demonstration, in costume.

Merry February! Nancy

fin janvier

Dear Mother:

Never let it be said that I lead a dull life. Last night Monique and I had donned pyjamas by 8:30 PM in order to study in comfort. The buzzer rang, once. We looked at each other in dismay, each clutching her striped flannelette and saying to the other, *"Mais je suis en pyjama!"* Since one ring theoretically designates Monique, she pulled a skirt and sweater over her pj top and barreled downstairs. In a minute she was up again and said, giggling furiously, that it was a tall, dark, handsome young man for me. But who? I got dressed, clattered downstairs and found Thierry-from-Grenoble. He had run away to Paris to find his muse.

Omigosh. I was in a panic.

This escapade, the very stuff of pulp romances, is alarming in real life unless, I suppose, the maiden is madly in love with her pursuer. The obligatory pleasantries (we spoke entirely in French) followed and then Thierry asked me out.

Nancy: *Désolée*, I cannot, *je suis occupée* (nervous cough).

Thierry (mournfully): But I will be leaving Paris early tomorrow!

Nancy: *Hélas*! It is regrettable, (etcetera, etcetera); and after the *de rigueur* farewell phrases, during which Thierry mentioned loftily that I could reach him at the George V, I disappeared upstairs. Monique, who was quite excited over the whole thing, latched the window in case he found a ladder and tried to climb in, like Julien Sorel in *le Rouge et le Noir*.[1]

The next morning early the buzzer rang, twice, and instinctively I knew it was Thierry. He hadn't left Paris yet and goodness knows where he'd really spent the night. ("Well", suggested Monique, "there **is** a George V métro stop.") Could he just use my room in order to shave?

The situation was getting beyond me, so in desperation I hailed the first male resident I saw (to whom I shall be forever grateful) and he led Thierry away, the latter saying hopefully, "*A tout à l'heure!*"

I grabbed my books and sped to the métro, determined to make it an all-day study session. I felt awfully hard-hearted but couldn't think of any other way to handle him. What would you have done? I am counting heavily on his having scant funds other than his return ticket to Grenoble; at any rate, touch wood, I've heard no more. But did you ever?

Yours unromantically,
Griselda

[1] Stendhal's 1830 novel of hopeless passion was required reading for French students.

2 février, evening

Dear Helen:

Mother's letter describing Kaye Leslie's arrival arrived in the post this evening. Dear family, I can't thank you enough for entertaining her so royally. Monique and Beth drooled when I described the roast lamb dinner.

WEEKLY CHRONICLE

Friday was a perfectly gorgeous, sunny day. In the afternoon, between classes, I explored the tiny, crooked, back streets in the *Quartier latin*[1] (my stroll was not entirely aimless; I had to pay rent for our radio at rue Claude-Bernard). The late afternoon sun, tinting all the

Receipt for the radio monthly rental, duly stamped and adorned with coupons.

buildings and winding, bumpy streets with saffron yellow, plus the soft, mild air, had brought everyone into the streets. There were little boys in blue pinafores (boys wear them here, up to the age of 9 or 10, over short trousers) romping about; and aproned merchants standing with folded arms in front of their shops. Neighbours called to each other from one dreary tenement to the next, animated by the fresh blue sky and unexpected, golden light. I felt very much a part of Paris and very happy. The *Quartier latin* is one of the oldest and most picturesque in Paris, though a sanitation and city planning expert would doubtless love to have the whole thing razed and reconstructed at the earliest possible chance.

Saturday—miracle of miracles—was another fine day, rendered even finer by a successful trip to the bank for a much-needed $35.00 (thank you, Papa). I lunched downtown in a little café near the Louvre and then headed for the Jardin des Tuileries where I sat in the sun for two hours, watching the shining green grass and the children playing. It had been my intention to see the Van Gogh exhibit at the Musée de l'Orangerie but I was waylaid by the enchanting weather. I eventually did make it to the Musée, which is at the opposite end of the Tuileries gardens; but found the exhibit disappointingly small. Later I found out that it wasn't meant to be a major exhibition at all, merely a special showing of the new Van Goghs which the Louvre had recently acquired.

That evening I went with Birgitta to the Olympia Music-hall and heard…Edith Piaf. She was marvellous. **Marvellous!** I can understand why she is Paris' Number 1 singer. She didn't DO anything, just came out on the stage in a simple, black dress and sang. Now the first half of the show consisted of a number of boffo acts but Edith Piaf did all the second half of the program herself and took the cake—really!

I haven't told you about Birgitta. She is engagingly frivolous, couldn't care less about Bach, Van Gogh, the French decadent poets or Baroque architecture and is thus a blessed relief. With her I can shelve my still unripe 'cultured' self without fear that it will be called to account at any moment.

Edith Piaf

The Olympia programme

Yesterday morning—Sunday—my American classmate Virginia and I made a pilgrimage to the famous *Marché aux Puces*.[2] The fine weather was over and an equally fine drizzle had set in, so that the Marché wasn't crowded. Never have I seen so many things I neither need nor want (as Daddy says whenever he enters a department store). What a lot of old junk: fans, porcelain boxes, sets of fruit knives, Chinese ash trays, buttons, antique furniture and even a fat, gilded Cupid, to be hung from the ceiling. He was about the size of a large turkey and equaled in bad taste only by a standing lamp consisting of two herons with their long necks twisted around each other, beaks gaping open.

I've just finished reading *Vol de nuit* by Antoine de St. Exupéry; it's a modern novel and terrific. France's inefficiency is redeemed by its literary genius.

On this upbeat note, please accept my most *respectueux sentiments*,

Nancy

---

[1] The Sorbonne and related Institutes which, from mediaeval times, are clustered in this area, once taught exclusively in latin—hence 'latin quarter'.

[2] Flea market

Saturday afternoon, early February

Dear Mom:

It's 5:50 PM and not dark. I can hardly believe it, after the weeks and weeks of winter night which descended around five. Right now I'm looking out my window at a patch of lovely blue sky. Today we've had rain and sun in intermittent bursts.

About an hour ago I laid aside *Gone With the Wind* (did you ever read such a rattling good story? I'll be sorry to finish it) and went daintily downstairs to see if there was any mail. I found a letter from you plus an invitation from the Maison canadienne to an art exhibition. Clutching both envelopes triumphantly I swept back upstairs, made a cup of Nescafé and…cut the first slice out of my brand-new Christmas cake. It arrived—it's lovely and moist—and the cookies weren't broken this time. It seems that packages are only delivered on Thursdays and yours came three Thursdays in succession. (I'm still suspicious. You mailed them in November. Why the big delay?)

The Franco-Britannique is holding a private entertainment on the evening of February 13th, in honour of Valentine's Day. Each floor (for once the men's side and the women's side are united) is to present a *tableau vivant* representing one of the métro stops. We, i.e. *le premier étage*,[1] are to present *Invalides*. I'm to be an armless old crone in a dressing gown, one sleeve flopping empty. Monique, if she can get permission from her parents to stay the weekend, is to be a nurse in a white apron and my tennis shoes which are about five sizes too big for her. Afterwards there'll be refreshments and dancing.

As for dancing, I'm invited to a *bal* in the Victor-Lyon House by Rhys, the Welsh lad who was part of our Christmas caroling group. Now, what shall I wear? I'm so fond of my new bracelet, the mashed pearls one which is also a necklace, that I think I'll wear a dress to go with it instead of the other way around.

As a corrective to all this frivolity, Mademoiselle *Vyk-ear* (that is how the French pronounce 'Wickwire') will sit a written phonetics exam on the 17th of February and an oral one on the 23rd or 24th.

The written part I think silly, because what good will it do me or my eventual students to be able to transcribe a French sentence like *Le chat est dans le jardin* into le lə ʃa e dã lə ʒaʀdɛ̃?[3] I feel confident about the oral… and, for my grand poetic recitation, have chosen a sonnet of Du Bellay's, (ahem!)

> *Heureux qui, comme Ulysse, a fait un beau voyage,*
> *Ou comme celui-là qui conquit le toison,*
> *Et puis est retourné, plein d'usage et raison,*
> *Vivre entre ses parents le reste de son âge!*
> *Etc.*

I've had a short letter from Peter Waite,[2] saying that he's coming to Europe again for the whole summer and, on his way to castles in Spain, will be passing through Paris and expects to see me. In May. Gosh! I must polish up my history.

Grandma has written as well, very worried about the Seine's flooding. The Halifax paper must have exaggerated as it wasn't serious and nobody was evacuated—at least, not in Paris.

On the worry front, Mamma dear, it will disturb you even more when I tell you that, when I was so sick with food poisoning, I **did** request a doctor AND HE DIDN'T COME. Also, I have booked another *audience* about my lack of monthly visitors (this despite the four injections into my bum), proving that I haven't entirely written off the French medical profession, though whether it's worth consulting is another matter.

France is braced for an epidemic of smallpox as I expect you've read in the news, and I may get vaccinated again just to make sure. For heaven's sake don't mention this to Grandma. So far the cases are confined to the south of France but all Europe has panicked as if it were the Black Death.

We are to have a new government. I asked one French lady about it and she said that, after all, Mendès France had been in office over six months now and it was bad for his health. And she was serious! We students think that Mendès fell because he allowed himself to be photographed drinking a glass of milk.

Love to all, Nancy

[1] 'the first floor', i.e. one level up. The ground floor is the *rez-de-chaussée*.

[2] Peter Waite, today a noted author and historian, was then a young history professor at Dalhousie University.

[3] Phonetic symbols, I discovered later, are invaluable for correct pronunciation.

Dear Mamma: *13 février, 3:00 PM*

SPECIAL BULLETIN

Two nights ago I was wined, dined and taken to the theater by our old family friend, Mr. Ed. Crawley.[1] Did you know he was coming to Paris?

In order to keep your breath bated I shall stop right there and tell you what else I've done lately.

Eh bien, last week I spent literally hours (muttering between my teeth) waiting in various lines to have my University of Paris-required medical. This consisted of an X-ray and a colour-blindness check, followed by a polite argument with a doubting doctor that yes, I was really left-handed; no, my parents hadn't tried to force me to use my right hand; yes, I'd write something for him just to prove it. I had a TB test and please tell Grandma that I got a smallpox vaccination.

At about the same time I began to get a funny tenderness in my left foot. By a week later it actually hurt to walk and this put me in a panic because, in Paris, you go everywhere *à pied*.[2] I thereupon betook myself to

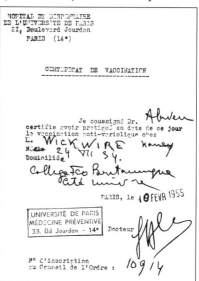

The precautionary vaccination anti-variolique (smallpox)

the clinic here at the Cité, where the harried staff refused even to look at it. *Merde!*

Undaunted—and in pain—I turned to M. LeMay, the director of the Maison canadienne. By luck he has a Canadian friend who is a foot doctor and who, that same day, examined the foot, diagnosed a mild case of bursitis and prescribed (a) soaking the foot in hot water and (b) wearing a special felt pad under the soles for

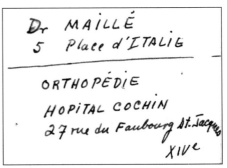

Dr MAILLÉ
5 Place d'ITALIE

ORTHOPÉDIE
HOPITAL COCHIN
27 rue du Faubourg St. Jacques
XIVe

M. Lemay sent me to his friend the orthopedic surgeon.

the sore spot (which was pressing down). I've been doing so and the foot is much better. Now, aren't Canadians great?

Tender foot and all, on Friday evening I went with an American fellow in my class named Timothy to see *les Diaboliques*, a film which is full of creepy suspense and all the rage in Paris—so much so that no one is supposed to tell the plot, not even newspaper reviewers: and no one is admitted to the cinéma in mid-film.

Anyway, when I got back to the Franco, there was a note in my box saying that a Monsieur Crawley had called and wished me to telephone him the next morning at the Hôtel Maintenon. Saturday morning dawned and, frustration of frustrations, I could find no Hôtel Maintenon in the entire Paris phone directory. As I was standing in the hall wondering what to do, the main door opened and there he was, as tweedy as ever. The Maintenon, it turns out, is in Versailles. Mr. Crawley said that he was leaving for London the next day but wished to escort me to dinner and a show that evening.

This made a really crammed day because I had previously invited Mme Donahoe, my phonetics teacher (she married an American, hence the name) to the Franco for tea. She exclaimed over the Christmas cake, which led me to saying how late arriving my Christmas parcels were. Madame Donahoe said darkly that postal clerks in France often 'put aside' interesting parcels until the official two months have elapsed when they can be pronounced 'lost'. She herself, when in the States, had sent a blouse to her mother as a birthday gift. It didn't arrive and, after three weeks, Madame D. initiated an inquiry through the U.S. postal service. Two days later *Maman* had her blouse.

Because of the tea party, I was dressed and ready when Mr. Crawley called. In a taxi (what grandeur) we went to the Hôtel du Louvre and had the 900-franc dinner each (curious dessert—a cake baked in a pie crust). We then hopped over to the Châtelet theatre to see the musical extravaganza *la Toison d'or* and had the seats usually reserved for M. Le Préfet de Police, in the first balcony. The operetta is really a series of glorious tableaux, ballets and songs, threaded together with a thin story which is the least important part. It was

wonderfully gay. Such costumes! First of all Swiss ones, then Turkish, Persian and Afghani in ever more gorgeous array. And such sets! All gold and red and blue. Sitting in that plushy seat I felt like a countess.

I had no trouble at all talking to Mr. Crawley in spite of the difference in our ages. He probably thought I chattered away like a birdbrain. I reminded him that he taught me my very first French words when we were living in Middleton (*un, deux, trois, quatre, cinq, six...*) he didn't remember, of course. Now my French is vastly better than his. When he gets back to Canada, please tell him how much I enjoyed seeing him.

On Sunday afternoon I went with Nouhé to a championship indoor tennis match, an invitation which I'd accepted days before or I'd have gone to bed instead. Anyway, the match was very good. First two women players played a singles, called *simple* in French: and then Budge Patty and somebody Stewart played the men's singles. Patty won, hands down.

Back home again, I got my *Invalides* costume ready and went downstairs to join our *tableau vivant* group. Our Napoleon was resplendent in greatcoat and paper 'Napoleon' hat and his two Imperial guards were gorgeously decked in paper vests, tall paper shakos with paper plumes, cardboard guns and (rented) tight, white breeches. An *ancien combattant*[3] carried the tricolore and the *mutilés de guerre*[4] all wore rows of military decorations on their jackets.

We saw at once that the other floors had worked much harder on their tableaux. *Franklin D. Roosevelt* was done up in western style with cowboys and Indians, a saloon, a Lady That's Known as Lou and the works. *Chemin-vert* was a bacchanalian scene featuring Bacchus complete with grapes, nymphs in Grecian draperies (sheets) carrying lyres and horns of plenty, plus satyrs and fauns, while *Pasteur* had amorous, 18th century shepherds and shepherdesses.

We all paraded, each group in turn, through the lounge and then downstairs to the *salle de récréation* where we arranged ourselves into tableaux while the vulgar mob and the judges gawked at us. To everyone's astonishment, ours won! According to the judges (all French), we came nearest to representing what we'd started out to represent while the others were simply gaudy, not to mention *immodeste*. We think we can attribute our victory to Napoleon—he is a sure vote-getter.

Be that as it may, we won and there was a dance afterwards, during which a fellow played a guitar and sang French songs. Altogether it was the most successful party of the year for the Franco.

So, today, I skipped classes and slept until noon. I'm really conked out!

Z-z-z-z-z-z-z-z-z, Nancy

[1] Mr. Crawley was a retired colleague of my father's.
[2] on foot
[3] war veteran
[4] war wounded

Invalides. (Monique as a nurse, Nancy with bandaged head.) We won!

Chemin-vert ('immodeste'). They lost.

Dear Mom:

How peaceful, just to sit and stare into space for a few minutes. I'm relishing our mardi gras holiday thoroughly though admittedly 'just sitting' hasn't entered into it much so far—in fact I've been on the tear for four days.

I'll explain about Saturday afternoon later and start with Saturday evening when Beth and I went to the British Embassy play, a dreadful thing of Shaw's called *The Simpleton of the Unexpected Isles.* The main attraction was that Tom (Beth's admirer) and Rhys (mine) were in it. They both loathe the play. After it was over the four of us kicked up our heels at the *bal masqué*[1] at the Maison canadienne, which lasted at least until 4:00 AM (which is when we left). It was *très gai* and full of odd people in surrealistic costumes—we wore masks but no costumes on account of having been to the Embassy.

Sunday evening I saw a very different play, *Ce cher Abel*, a comedy performed by the Théâtre Monceau, one of the tiny art theatres—and as funny as can be, well-cast and acted to perfection. I understand nearly everything, even, thanks to Monique, the slang. I went with Rhys who has absurdly developed a crush on me. He's awfully nice, apart from that, and in fact I once inadvertently called him 'Duncan' by mistake, which is just as well, because the fellows here try to brand a girl as 'theirs' once they've been out with her a few times and this particular gal is determined to resist romantic entanglements while so far from hearth, country and flag.

This evening, attired in my red jumper (called a pinafore dress by the Brits), I betook myself to the Théâtre Gramont to see *le Héros et le Soldat*, a translation of *Arms and the Man*. Nicole Pouzargues met me at the theatre and we had a little loge all to ourselves. It was really well-performed. Shaw seems to lend itself better to translation than Shakespeare (I'm thinking of *Macbeth*). This winter Paris is crazy about English and American plays, they occupy every stage, all translated into French, of course.

As today is Shrove Tuesday, I threw a breakfast party, the only fly in the butter (real butter for the occasion) being the *femme de chambre* [2] who kept wanting to clean the room. I'd presumed she's have a mardi gras holiday too but I was wrong. The *invitées* were Beth Ogilvie, Jean Logsden (from South Africa, preparing a thesis on the poet Paul Eluard) and, surprise, surprise, Dorothy Yates, about whom I'll explain in a minute. I'd decorated the room with red and yellow crepe paper streamers and masks. We gabbed away and had a lovely time.

Now, about Saturday afternoon and Dorothy. She phoned me from the 'Y' just after lunchtime, having arrived that second from Montauban with a whole week off and starving for Paris' museums and theatres. Twenty minutes later we were entering the Louvre together, where I fear we talked more than we looked; but at any rate we went through the motions of bestowing favoured glances upon Egyptian and Assyrian statues.

While we were there, a dear, chubby old man approached us and asked, in good English, if we could show him the way out of this labyrinth? We pointed in the direction of the exit but he began to chat instead, in a mixture of French and English, about his travels, how he kept young by going to museums and lectures, about his daughters (all, we gathered, wed to noblemen), what a wonderful country is Canada, a brief sketch of his life beginning with his grandfather and, finally, he gave us each his card, with the expressed intention of taking us to a concert anytime we should care to call on an old man.

Dot and I escaped and collapsed in laughter behind the nearest marble pillar. After collecting our Anglo-Saxon dignity we were busy inspecting coy Venuses in another hall when whom should we spy coming towards us with a young girl in tow, talking earnestly and delightedly? Our old man! I suppose he spends all his afternoons giving out cards to people.

I then had a brilliant idea. Since *Don Juan* was playing right here at the Cité on Monday night, I suggested to Dot that she come for supper Monday, see the play and stay overnight in Monique's bed (highly illegal, of course). Dorothy, who is as charming and giddy as ever, accepted—and that is how she was in on the breakfast party. *Don Juan*, by the way, was marvellous. It's the familiar Don Giovanni story with the moving statue, etc. and is, I believe, Molière's only prose play. I understood every word.

And that's how *mardi gras* was celebrated by,

Yours truly, Nancy B.Vyk-ear

[1] masked ball
[2] chambermaid

February 23

Dear Mamma:

Eh bien, we've been living without a government for eighteen days now and if M. Edgar Faure doesn't succeed this afternoon with his program we're liable to go for several days more. Faure is generally expected to succeed. People say that Mendès France was overthrown principally because he was getting too popular and, since elections are coming up soon (within the year, I think) all the Radicals and Radical-Socialists and Peasants and Communists and MRPs [1] were afraid he would sweep the country and they and their precious parties would be rendered impotent. Others say, No, that Mendès fell because of his stupidity regarding the Algerian question.[2] Since every deputy in the Assembly seems to be there for his own gain and pocket as far as I can see (*moi*, the untutored foreigner), the first reason has a good gob of truth in it.

Paul Claudel [3] died last night. I remember studying his poems in school. It seems funny to be living at the same time as famous writers as, until now, I've had the fixed idea that to be a celebrated author automatically presupposes that one has been dead at least a hundred years.

♡, Nancy

P.S. Duncan writes me that T.V. is getting a death-grip on Halifax audiences. True or false? Have you bought one yet?

Hugs, Nancy

[1] Mouvement Républicain Populaire

[2] Algeria was erupting in violence in its quest for independence from France.

[3] French lyric poet, playwright and diplomat, 1868-1955. His sister, Camille Claudel, was a sculptor whom some consider Rodin's equal.

Feb. 28

✒ *From a letter to Duncan*

. . . Paul Claudel is dead and no one is letting us forget it. I was half going to go to his funeral this morning but decided against as it was so cold out. None of this prevents the critics from slashing his play *l'Annonce faite à Marie* which recently opened at the Comédie-Française and which Claudel directed himself. People say it's awful.

The big fashion houses have issued their dictates. Ah, Dior! Ah, Patou! Ah, Balenciaga! We ladies, this spring, will have the choice of looking like this:

or like this:

either way, hopelessly and permanently deformed.

Monday, Feb. 28

✒ Dear Mom:

Well, it happened. My little Welshman Rhys *s'est déclaré*,[1] as the French say. This is really too bad as he is so easy to talk to and now we can't continue as comrades. Saturday night we went to a western-style hop at the Fondation des Etats-Unis and did the hoe-down with scads of cowboys, Indians and Annie Oakleys plus a few sirens who preferred to wear their slinky black cocktail dresses. It was in a little café across the boulevard Jourdan, after the dance, that Rhys made his proposal of marriage. I refused as gently as I could, making large mention of Duncan and saying that I was sailing for Canada on July 1. Oh, dear.

British males have an entirely different attitude towards women than do North American ones. At home, men seem to flee any suggestion of permanent attachment—over here, chaps practically beg girls to tie them down. I, the callous Canadian, ascribe it to a lack of experience with women—British men really should know better. Mind you, if I were to fall in love, it would be different. But I haven't. Isn't it funny how love can be one-sided? 'Til now I have cherished the notion that it necessarily worked both ways, always. I'm afraid that deep down inside I attribute his passion to youth and Paris and so on and figure he'll get over it. Also I'm flattered no end, if I must be truthful.

The next night, i.e. Sunday, I went to the Théâtre National Populaire to see *Cinna*, by Corneille. This time I didn't understand a WORD. What a setback! But now, I ask you, am I more to be pitied or censured? *Cinna* is a severely classical drama, set in ancient Rome. There is no action to speak of, instead, each actor comes forward and declaims his long, heroic speech in classical alexandrines. On glancing over the text, which I'd tried to plough through Sunday afternoon, I found it full of anguished, mental struggles…oh, well, at least I've seen a classical drama. I went with Timothy, who took me out to dinner first. We ate in a quaint little restaurant just off the boul' Mich'—had pork chops with tomato and for dessert, a *crêpe*. A French mardi gras special, the crêpe! It's an enormous, tissue-thin pancake which comes folded into a half-moon. You spoon jam onto one-quarter of the moon and then roll it all up like a cornucopia and eat it with a knife and fork. It's good but ever so filling and would have done me nicely without the pork chop.

It's As Ye Sow So Shall Ye Reap time at the Sorbonne. Friday afternoon we had the first of our two oral phonetics exams. I waited from 2:00 PM until 5:00 PM to take mine because, in typical French fashion, they'd passed out numbers to us as we came in (mine was 13, horrors!) and, in typical Anglo-Saxon fashion, I thought that we would take the exam in numerical order. By the time I woke up to the fact that it was First Come, First Served, it was 4:00 and I had to get into the queue like everybody else. The exam itself consisted of my reading a text from Gide which they handed me as I entered and then holding a sort of artificial conversation with the three examiners. By the time my conversation was over, they were answering my questions and I got out as quickly as I could, hoping they didn't think I'd pulled a fast one. Part two was on Saturday morning and consisted of the recitation of *Heureux qui, comme Ulysse,* my poem. Wise now, I got there early and was second in line. The words seemed to flow out of my mouth easily and I sank gratefully afterwards into a boul' Mich' café, quite confident of passing.

To be truthful, I'm writing this letter in bed because I've been sick to my stomach again. Isn't that strange? Both Sunday evenings when I ate out in quaint little restaurants I was sick Monday. This time, though, thanks to a continuous diarrhea, I've got the offending material out of my body and feel much revived.

POLITICAL REPORT

Les accords de Paris[2] have been ratified in Bonn—so the number of students handing out pamphlets and shouting, "*Contre le réarmement de l'Allemagne!*"[3] has ballooned. Are they truly *engagés*[4] or just skipping classes? I must ask Monique.

Until the next bulletin, your Paris correspondent,
N. Wickwire, signs off.

[1] 'declared himself', i.e. proposed.
[2] The Accords ended Allied occupation of West Germany and allowed limited German rearmament.
[3] Against German rearmament!
[4] dedicated

March 7

Dear Mom:

Big news! Thanks to André Gide I've advanced from section *2* to section 1 in the school. (I may have already written you this but I'll repeat it out of sheer vanity.) To celebrate, I splurged and bought two Vermeer reproductions: *The Lacemaker* and *Girl with a Pearl Necklace*.

The colours are so warm and look at home on our walls which are a buff tone. I love them—Vermeer is my current favourite.

Yesterday (Sunday) I didn't get up 'til almost eleven and after a quick lunch took a bus to the Comédie-Française. Sunday afternoons there's always a matinee and this time they were performing *le Barbier de Séville*.[1] I got there three-quarters of an hour before the wicket opened and the queue was already blocks long. By the time I got to the head of the line (as I wasn't bored waiting either, as the fellow and girl in front of me spend their time embracing madly) there was nothing left but the 40-franc seats. That's about 13 cents. I decided to take one just to see how bad they were. I went up...up...up to the very roof or what the French call *le poulailler* and this is what I saw: about one-third of the lower left-hand side of the stage. I snickered to myself and sneaked out, to the consternation of the *ouvreuses*,[2] who thought I was sick.

The afternoon was far from spoiled though, because when I got back to the Franco I ran into Tui Flower and invited her to tea in my room. Tui is from New Zealand and, since she is here studying French cooking and is a home economics expert, we talked about the French and their superiority complex re: food. Tui, completely unimpressed, thinks that French cooking is very limited. According to her, they have only three kinds of pastry mixture, it's made into different shapes, that's all. They are addicted to olive oil and pour it over everything. Every single cake, no matter what its name, is doused with rum. She is firmly convinced that the French neither know nor care a fig about scientific nutrition (and it's true, you know, that the foods for which France is famous are all bad for you!)

After disposing of the French and their cuisine, we discussed possibilities for the long Easter holiday and ended up deciding to visit the Scandinavian countries. Whaddyathink? There's a night train to Copenhagen (Tui has friends in Denmark) and we could go on to Sweden, then Norway and return through Holland. If we depart on April 2 we could return on the 16th or 17th. Good *idée?*

Describing my week chronologically backwards: Saturday night I stepped into my high-necked purple velvet and went to the Moulin Rouge with Marc-Antoine. Frankly, I was disappointed. The Moulin Rouge is not a real nightclub, more like a smoky music-hall decorated in the worst possible taste, filled with as many tables and chairs as can possibly be crammed in (are there any fire regulations here?) and a tiny stage which juts out into the audience. The whole point of going is to see the show—which I considered mediocre. Even the can-can girls hadn't the snap of Dalhousie's can-can line. It's true! To cap it all, I'd already seen a lot of the acts a month ago, at l'Olympia. Anyway, afterwards we went to a *dancing* where we twirled until 4:30 A.M. I was dead! The *boîte* was packed with young French people all dressed up in their dancing finery. 'Hm-m-m-m,' I thought, 'how different is their taste!' At home, a girl has to have clean hair, a clean neck and fingernails and hairless underarms—but not in France. It was I, fastidiously scrubbed and shaved, who was the alien. Sigh.

I have now definitely decided that I am one of those Morning People. I love going out for the evening but after 1:00 AM at the latest I'm a chewed string. I did have fun Saturday night as after all, Paris is Paris: but I also continue to discover things about myself.

Let's see. What else have I found out? I finally went to the doctor because my most recent bout of indigestion wasn't clearing up and got into quite a lively argument with his assistant, whose job it was to ask, as one comes in, what one wants, etc. I explained in words of one syllable that my *estomac* wasn't working properly, I couldn't eat and I couldn't go to classes and I wanted the doctor to give me something to cure this indisposition. He shrugged his Gallic shoulders. 'What do you want him to give you?' he asked in French, in an annoyed voice. A couple of months ago I'd have burst into frustrated tears but now, I take no guff. "How'm I supposed to know? *Je ne suis pas médicin, moi!*" I retorted in my best nasal accents. This seemed to satisfy him, as I was sent immediately to the doctor and given immense carbon pills which cleared up my tum immediately.

Rhys continues to hang around and is getting to be rather a bother. Your daughter likes young men but, so far, a certain Mr. Fraser seems the only chap who doesn't get tiresome after a while. *Mais comment faire comprendre à ces gens? Ils sont impossibles, ces Britanniques!*[3]

I saw *le Rouge et le Noir* this afternoon, with Gérard Philipe, the French teen-agers' idol. We studied the novel at Dal. (On re-reading this paragraph I must hastily assure you that Monsieur Philipe did not accompany me to the cinéma; he starred in the film, wherein he climbs into his lady-love's bedroom on a ladder.) Hopeless love is the theme: does it not sound familiar?

The students in section 1 must write an essay about *Un souvenir d'enfance.*[4] I've written about our blackberry-picking trips to Katen Sand Beach (or 'Cake-and-Sandwich', har, har) on the Bay of Fundy. I described the parti-coloured toadstools we'd collect and the Canada jays and the electric fence and the insects which danced on the surface of the brook, the steep path down to the shore, the driftwood fire—we did have good times, didn't we?

Good-night, sweet dreams, Nancy

[1] Beaumarchais' 1775 comedy was later immortalized in opera form by Rossini.
[2] ushers
[3] But how can one make these chaps understand? Brits are impossible!
[4] A childhood memory

8 mars, 1955

Dear Sugar Daddy:

Let me come directly to the point. I want—no, I would like—no, I shall need, my March ration of pocket money doubled. Please? Because for the Easter holiday I am going on a fabulous train trip to Denmark and Sweden with Tui Flower. She and I went to various travel agencies this afternoon and came home loaded with pamphlets, maps and all the dope. We want to leave Paris April 2, go to Copenhagen, stay there most of a week, then on to Stockholm, Oslo and Bergen; from Bergen we can take an overnight boat to Rotterdam and the train back to Paris. The transportation by various trains and boats (all

Third Class) will come to about $100.00. With my remaining traveller's cheques and your February and March bank drafts I'll have $220.00; add to this half my April bourse money plus some money I've saved and I'll have about $275.00. This should do it nicely as we intend to take the inexpensive hotels; but, but, I'd hate to be stranded on a Norwegian fjord without a *sou* and one never knows what may turn up in the way of unexpected expenses. So, if you could send me $70.00 in March I'd be grateful.

Tui and I had great fun at the travel agencies. At Bennett's the clerk had to be pumped for each scrap of information and when he found we intended to travel steerage, so to speak, he totally lost interest. Fortunately it was one of my good days for speaking French so I was able to bully a few maps from him.

Next we went to the Norwegian travel agency where we met a charming Norwegian fellow who couldn't understand why we wanted to go to Norway in April and tried to discourage us. It appears that hordes of skiers flock to both Norway and Sweden at Easter-time and thus it's awfully hard to get rooms. I asked him whether it would be more advantageous to take French francs or American dollars. "Oh", he said, rather embarrassed and quite cautiously, "Oh, well, I can't really say; I'm quite neutral, you see," as if we'd asked him whether he were **for** or **against** the Republic.

We bursary students are on a tight lead vis-à-vis our residence in France. We are allowed two weeks total in another European country during the school year—if we exceed that our bursaries are cancelled. This is to discourage the giddy who might otherwise plan to use their whole year travelling about Europe.

I've been reading heaps of material this evening. If we go to Holland we should just hit the tulip season. Since we hope to disembark at Rotterdam at about 8:00 in the morning, we can easily go to Delft which is the city of my darling Vermeer and only about a centimetre away on the map.

Monique is lucky to be out this evening seeing the French version of Graham Greene's *Living Room*, because I have just eaten three apples, not having had enough supper, and am beginning to make *des pets* (very smelly) all over the place. I skimped on supper because we were having French fries. Again. At first I liked them but we get served them so often that now I can't stand the sight of the things. And that was our Main Dish this evening!

Skoal! Nancy

March 12

Dear Parents:

Oh, what a rogue and peasant slave am I! Daddy has a birthday and what does he get in the mail? A request for seventy dollars! Please forgive me and accept my compliments on the day, Sire; and I hope you got a chocolate cake.

Maria wrote me from her posting in Sicily. She left Grenoble the 15th of February and traveled to Venice and Rome first. She finds the Sicilian baroness very kind but the little boy a perfect terror. The Adelphi School requires that she write a paper on *The Italian Family*. Since this one is hardly typical, being the richest family in all Sicily, I don't know how she is to manage—I only know that, being Maria, she will, somehow. I also got a cheerful letter from Grandma, addressed 'College Franco-Britannique, Paris'. It was sent all over the city before finally getting here.

This afternoon I went via métro to an orchestral concert (5:30 to 7:30) and heard wonderful Brahms and Tchaikovsky, whose names I can now spell. Shall I impress you even further? Last Thursday evening there was a harpsichord concert here at the Cité, given by an old, old lady who looked about as antique as the instrument. She was a darling, wispy and timid, hardly daring to take a bow afterwards—but what surprising strength in her fingers! I was afraid I'd go mad if I sat through a whole evening of harpsichord but she was superb and I enjoyed the whole thing from start to finish. Her name was Wanda Landowska.[1]

Yesterday I trotted off with Timothy to see the film version of *Knock*,[2] a play by Jules Romains which we studied at Dal. Tim is an intellectual aesthete who lives in a real garret but, oh dear! Why does spring make a young man's fancy turn to thoughts of? After the film we strolled along the Seine to the Jardin des Plantes which is both a biological garden and a zoo. We didn't visit the garden but did see the animals, arriving at the lion and tiger cages just as the beasts were being fed hunks of raw meat. What magnificent things! I don't know how they can be kept in such good condition in captivity. There was only one tiger but he was a beaut—all stripy and with a 'Tiger, tiger, burning bright' sort of face.

Among the endless specimens was a curious species of goat which, the plaque stated, come in three colours: *noir, blanc* and *isabelle*. It appears that a certain Queen Isabelle vowed not to change her shift until the king conquered Grenada. Well, the war went on for three years before the king was finally victorious, by which time the shift was a creamy coffee colour. Hence a goat *isabelle* is a sort of in-between, coffee brown!

Tim is a good egg, I like him a lot, but when he attempted to put his manly arm about my delicate shoulders I politely shrugged away and, having already had lunch with him, declined a dinner invitation-cum-visit to his garret on the (fictitious) grounds that Monique and I had plans for the evening. Really, I wish that they wouldn't. It spoils everything.

Yours in purity, Nancy

[1] Celebrated Polish-French musician (1879-1959) who restored the popularity of the harpsichord as a concert instrument.
[2] Romains' 1923 farce mocks the insidious power of contemporary advertising.

March 16

Dear Helen:

Thank you for sending the peanut butter and the cookies. (Are they peanut butter cookies, by any chance?) The parcel ain't here yit but we now know that the average delay is three weeks.

I had breakfast downstairs in the Franco common room with Sarasu, who is in fine fettle. She has fallen in love with an American

boy in her class and in order to stay here with him for another year
(I think they plan to get married), she has applied for an extension of
her *bourse*. Sara revealed her personal tragedy to me over coffee.
Though a Protestant and educated in English private schools, she is
from Ceylon, whither she returned after graduating from Cambridge,
only to find that her parents had selected a husband for her. He was
very old and ugly, she says, and she refused to obey, causing a nasty
cultural scandal. She was sent to Paris so her family could save face.
Well, I hope this will lead to happiness for her though one can foresee
rocks ahead.

It's nice to go down for breakfast occasionally, if one has oodles
of time, because one always meets lots of friends. The downside is, that
breaking bread there usually adds up to oodles of francs, so I restrict
the treat.

My being advanced into Section 1 is a Good Thing as it means
my grammar and composition courses are more challenging and I'm
treated as an university and not a high-school student. And, I found
out my promotion is due not to *Heureux qui, comme Ulysse* but to the
grammar and composition exams I wrote in February. Phonetics, it
seems, is a thing apart.

We've had two warm days in succession and there is one tree by
the Argentine House with great big, fat buds, just itching to burst
open. The nicest thing about winter is that spring comes right after.

Your sister has finally gone skating in Paris. The rink is open-air
and has artificial ice which is theoretically great, except that the ice
wasn't cleaned off once so by 10:00 PM we were blade-deep in slush.
And there wasn't any music! Never mind, it felt splendid to be on
skates again. Now in Canada, one is carried around the rink by a
stream of expert skaters going sixty miles an hour. Here everyone was
a beginner and there was much falling down and laughing. There was
even one bare-legged glamour girl who teetered onto the ice togged
out in a tiny black velvet skirt with fur trim and a blue satin lining. In
France, appearances are EVERYTHING.

I've started dreaming again. I'd completely stopped after getting off the boat. Perhaps the inner eye or whatever, was trying to get adjusted to being in France and speaking French? Now I'm dreaming furiously as if to make up for lost time, and in French, too. I feel I've arrived.

Here's a good story about the Princess Margaret and Captain Townsend situation.[1] The French take it quite seriously and one of the *femmes de chambre*[2] is reported as saying:

Vous verrez! Quand Churchill est mort, ça sera la fin de la monarchie anglaise! Vous verrez comme j'ai raison! Et la Princesse Margaret, qui va se marier avec un divorcé. C'est terrible. Vous verrez! Elle se mariera et puis elle va **abdiquer** *comme le roi Edouard VII!*[3]

Dorothy Yates sent me a little gift of Toulouse *violette* perfume. The bottle is ever so sweet with a little velvet violet attached to it but the scent is quite overpowering. Actually, along with urine and garlic, it is one of the principal odours of the Paris métro.

Luv, Nancy

[1] War hero Peter Townsend was equerry to King George VI when the teen-aged Margaret fell in love. She was determined to marry him and could do so without Royal consent once she reached age 25. As Townsend was Roman Catholic, divorced and twice her age, Parliament vetoed the match—unless the Princess renounced all her Royal privileges. Margaret capitulated in October 1955.

[2] chambermaid

[3] You'll see! When Churchill dies, that'll be the end of the British monarchy! You'll see how right I am! And Princess Margaret, who's going to marry a divorced man! It's terrible! You'll see! She'll marry and then she'll abdicate, like King Edward the Seventh (sic)!

March 23, afternoon

Dear Family:

It's Monday, it's spring and ever since the equinox we've had wet mornings and warm, blue, sunshiny afternoons. For the first time I feel chilly in the métro instead of suffocatingly hot. It's actually warmer outdoors.

Saturday after breakfast I hied myself out to a massive exhibit called *les Arts ménagers*. It was due to close Sunday so I just managed to squeak in. All the big expositions are at the Grand Palais, an enormous edifice consisting of a central, vaulted hall with two mezzanines running around it. I toddled in (only 150 francs in the morning) and what a colossal salvo of advertisements greeted me! All the refrigerator companies, all the vacuum cleaner companies, the water heaters, the wine bottlers, cheese makers, furniture companies, soap, boot polish, cutlery and stove purveyors were there in force, each with shouting sales demonstrators and gaudy neon signs. In the furniture section were entire rooms decorated either in ultra-modern style or (much preferred by Monique who went last week) with antique period furniture. In my opinion the latter were stuffy and cluttered, I far and away preferred the modern rooms. While gazing at the period displays, though, I heard exclamations of admiring approval from all sides. The French seem automatically to associate gilt and carving with ease and wealth. Afterwards I simply had to buy a little baked cheese tart, hot from the oven. The smell of those tarts filled the whole enormous exhibition building.

From here I went by métro to my rendez-vous with a footwear correction specialist, the doctor at the Cité having arranged for her to make me a special insole for my left shoe (the foot still bothers me a little). Now it happened that just opposite her studio there was a dingy little *coiffeur* shop which advertised a plain cut for 200 francs. The price was just up my alley so I penetrated (there's no other word for it) the shop. They were busy but could take me in half-an-hour. *Entendu!* [1] As le Bazar de l'Hôtel de Ville [2] was right next door, I wedged myself into the crowd and elbowed rudely about (*Pardon!* shove) until I found the alcohol stove section (our old stove was literally on its last three legs). *Voilà,* a magnificent model for only 490 francs, so I bought it and returned to the *coiffeur.* It was as crowded as ever but having nothing else to do I sat and watched as two jolly ladies had their hairs dyed—one, jet black and the other, red. Everyone was gay and chatty and by five o'clock my hair was stylishly cut and I was swinging merrily across the Seine with warm sun in my eyes, and all the way along the boul' Mich' to the Luxembourg métro. I felt completely, totally happy. Maybe it was the new haircut? Or maybe it was just spring.

Later I talked to my American friend Virginia who also went to the *Arts ménagers*. While in front of the refrigerator displays, she overheard disdainful French comments about this apparatus, another American frivolity it seems, like Coca-cola and chewing gum. A *grand'mère* remarked knowingly, 'You put food in it, *oui, bon,* but it goes RIGHT ON SPOILING.'

Not every student house is as puritanical as the Franco-Brit., as I've just found out. A friend of Beth's named Michelle lives in Fondation Deutch de la Meurthe where men and women are allowed at any time in each other's rooms. Michelle has often found her roommate entertaining male visitors on either her own or on Michelle's bed. Michelle finds this *impoli.*[3] I giggled and concurred but, myself, would have used a stronger adjective.

Like a fool I washed my hair (oops, hairs!) late this afternoon and put it in pincurls. Now I'll have to eat supper in my room as it's not dry yet and one cannot go into the Maison internationale dining room with any kind of bandanna or headgear, or everyone shouts *cha-peau! cha-peau! cha-peau!* and bangs on the table until you take it off. This sort of juvenile persecution is an especial torment for Sikhs who have to wear their turbans at all times. When a Sikh student comes into the dining-room the racket is deafening and doesn't cease until the poor man has eaten and fled.

And finally, thank you, Daddy, for the extra money.

Much love, Nancy

[1] Right you are!
[2] A department store on the rue de Rivoli, noted for its enormous hardware department.
[3] impolite

mailed in late March

✒ *From a letter to Duncan*

Remember, one evening before I sailed, you remarked that people seem either to love Paris and never want to leave, or hate it and want to go home right away? I wonder where I fit in? Sometimes I execrate the place, especially when I'm tired (and I'm tired a lot). Other times I'm enchanted by it and mourn the fact that, in July, I'll have to leave all this for good. I then muse to myself, 'Even if I do stay, I'd hate it the second year—it's like having two desserts, the first one is delicious, the second, sickening.'

Dorothy Yates came to Paris from Montauban for mardi gras and said that she wishes now she'd stayed only the one year and then gone home.

Peter Waite thinks I'm daft to return to Canada in July. He is going to spend the whole summer in Spain and Switzerland. We Canadians are educated to revere everything European and admittedly, I still do, it's just that living here has knocked a lot of the romance out of me. If I've learned one thing since coming, though, it's that you meet exactly the same problems and have the same inner resources to deal with them whether you're in Paris or Musquodoboit, Nova Scotia.

27 mars

✒ Dear Mamma:

It's twenty past eleven of a wet, mild Sunday morning. I'm a-sitting at my work table, having just finished plowing through *Polyeucte* and *Horace*, both by Corneille, because on Tuesday we've got to hand in a *rédaction*[1] on *Le héros cornélien*.[2] I swear his heroes crib each other's speeches. After reading so much alexandrine verse my brain swimmeth in rhyming couplets. For example:

> *Ma chère, douce Mère, je veux t'écrire un mot,*
> *Te rassurer un peu, éviter tes sanglots,*
> *Ma santé est parfaite, mon bonheur assuré,*
> *Mon travail même brille, mes amies bonnes et gaies.*[3]

To make it scan you've got to pronounce the e's which are underlined. This sort of rhythmic cheating is permitted in French and helps the poet reel off verses without much effort.

The tree outside our window is fuzzy with greenish catkins. It's a pretty sturdy tree and I understand that Friday evening, it served as a pedestal for a Peeping Tom who suddenly got the urge to look into our bedrooms.

Marc-Antoine is going home to Ottawa on Wednesday. It seems he has had a sort of nervous breakdown so his parents sent him money to return. Two Saturdays ago he'd invited me to a dance at the Maison canadienne but an evening with Marc-Antoine is so mentally and physically wearing that I'd politely declined. Then I learned from John Clark that he was leaving for good! This made me feel remorseful so I dropped in to see him last Tuesday. Well, well—*figure-toi* [4]—the dance had been switched to the following Saturday, i.e. last night. I couldn't refuse this time. Marc-Antoine brought me a bunch of miniature daffodils and two tiny books of poetry. Fancy! I put the daffodils in water and off we went.

For the first time I felt my French was superior to his English. We spoke in French all evening. Previously it's been a fight between the Academic Me—desperately determined to *parler français*—and the Comradely Me, resorting to English in order to be understood. All in all the evening was most successful and Marc-Antoine asked me out to dinner Tuesday evening.

This afternoon Jean Logsden and I, rain or no rain, are going to see *l'Amour des quatre Colonels*. [5] The theatre is miles away. It takes at least an hour to get there so we'll have to board the métro at 1:30 to be on time for the show at 3:00.

The forsythia in front of the Mexican House is *en fleurs* [6] and last Friday afternoon I picked marguerites on the lawn behind the Franco. A few daffodils in the sunny corner behind the Collège F-Brit are yellow with bloom. Oh, what weather! Virginia Johnson and I buy cheese and bread and eat lunch in the Jardin du Luxembourg instead of going to the dark old Foyer International.

SUNDAY EVENING

The Marigny is a tiny little theatre and means a long, tiresome ride on the métro but *l'Amour des quatre Colonels* was well worth it. It was super. I laughed and wept and philosophized. We had really good seats and the theatre creates instant intimacy because of its size. The four colonels were beautifully played and every detail was exact, down to the American, Russian and British accents. It was worth twenty métro rides. I think Jean enjoyed it but since it is in her philosophical nature to be mournful, I'm still not sure.

Theatrically yours,

Nancy

[1] essay

[2] Corneille's heros

[3] *'My dear sweet Mother, I wish to drop you a line,*
Reassure you a bit, prevent your sobs,
My health is perfect, my happiness assured,
My work even shines, my girlfriends good and gay.'

[4] guess what!

[5] Peter Ustinov's play, set in postwar Germany, opened in London in 1951. Four colonels representing the U.S.A., Britain, France and Russia, are frustrated with stalemated political negotiations, so each in turn fantasizes about his Ideal Woman.

[6] in bloom

VERNISSAGE
(ready to show the world)

April 2 to July 1

From **BRITANNICA BOOK OF THE YEAR, 1955**

APRIL

April 5: Sir Winston Churchill resigned as prime minister of the United Kingdom.

April 6: Queen Elizabeth II of the United Kingdom named Sir Anthony Eden to succeed Sir Winston Churchill as prime minister.

April 12: Anti-poliomyelitis vaccine developed by Dr. Jonas E. Salk was revealed to be effective against paralytic polio upon the basis of field trials in 44 states.

MAY

May 2: Columbia University announced the award of the 1954 Pulitzer prizes, including one to Tennessee Williams for his play Cat on a Hot Tin Roof and one to William Faulkner for his work A Fable.

May 16: King Baudouin of Belgium arrived in Léopoldville for a 27-day visit to the Belgian Congo.

May 19: French cabinet approved measures for increasing the strength of French armed forces in Algiers.

May 31: U.S. Supreme Court in an unanimous decision directed the states to end racial segregation in public schools within a reasonable time.

JUNE

June 9: British royal commission recommended major land reforms in Kenya, Tanganyika and Uganda and a pattern for future land development.

Dear Daddy:

Yesterday was April Fool's Day but nobody pulled any jokes on me. I missed it! Did you escape or were there 'soup stains on your tie' or 'razor cuts on your chin' as usual?

I'm writing while lying at full length on the lawn behind the Franco, on—not in—my coat. The sun is so warm and the grass smells so good. I feel very happy because Tui and I are leaving Paris tonight. It's like shedding a dusty cocoon.

Yesterday, as I have already stated, was April Fool's Day and classes were cancelled, not as a joke but because Easter hols begin tomorrow. To celebrate, Nouhé and I went, at 4:00 PM, to see a Japanese film called *Yokasan*. We were impressed by the quality. It was simple and tender, set in post-war Tokyo and was a series of sketches of the life of an average family seen through the eyes and mind of a child of around fourteen.

And yester-evening, Beth, Sarasu, Jean Logsden, Jane Henry and Tui Flower came for after-dinner coffee *chez moi*. I had to borrow cups and chairs from my guests—a most ungracious thing anywhere but the Cité universitaire. The prospect of two whole weeks of holiday having rendered us a little mad, the party went on until rather late. To go with the coffee we munched some chocolate fish and snails which are traditionally eaten in France on April 1. *Poisson d'avril*[1] is their equivalent of April Fool's Day. After they left I still had to wash my hair, pack, etcetera but really I was too excited to sleep anyway.

The previous day's classes were cancelled, too. It was sunny and fresh so I decided to skip out of dirty, noisy Paris to the woods around, bought a 30-franc ticket and rattled away all by myself to the Parc de Sceaux. When I got off the train everything was so quiet and the air smelt good. The Parc surrounds a beautiful little château which belonged to the brother of Louis XIV (I think). The grounds roll downhill towards a long, rectangular pool with three swans swimming and tall poplar trees all around, in full bud. I sat down under one of them and enjoyed the sunshine. There were violets in the grass if you looked hard, purple harebells, a few rare buttercups and, in front of the château, the lawns were white with early daisies, called *pâquerettes* because they bloom for Easter, *Pâques*. The grass shone like clean hair. Oh, it was so different from Paris, so lovely. I don't think I could stand living another year in a huge, dirty metropolis, even a Canadian one. I'm not urban at heart, it seems.

Have you ever read anything by John Dos Passos? I'd never heard of him before coming here but he and Hemingway are all the rage with French students studying American writers. In order not to appear a moron, I bought and read *The 42nd Parallel*. It pictures an America I never knew and barely recognize, the America of 1910; yet it's that America which Europeans think still exists in 1955.

Well, I've tried to pack everything into one small suitcase but it won't work, especially if I want any room for souvenirs of Scandinavia, so I'm lugging two. I'm going to wear slacks and and pack my grey suit, pyjamas, underwear and toilet stuff. That's ALL. They always say, 'Take half the clothes you think you'll need' but I can't very well take half of that or I'll be recruited by one of those Swedish nudist colonies. Golly. I do hope it won't be too cold. Anyhow I'm prepared for anything except a real heat wave.

Happy Easter from your European butterfly and love to everyone,

Nancy

---

[1] 'April fish!' The tease is, to pin a paper fish on someone's back without his noticing.

April 4, KFUK,
St. Kanniskaestrade 19, Copenhagen

Dear Mom:

Here we are in a little room at the Copenhagen YWCA (KFUK, if you please). It's clean as clean and cheap as cheap. Tui and I couldn't care if it were the very opposite as we're bushed as bushed.

To back up: We boarded the overnight train out of Paris and rumbled northward through Belgium into Germany. I suppose we only crossed three borders but with all the passport inspections it seemed like twenty-three. If we'd splurged on a sleeper we shouldn't have used it much. Every few miles another *pass-control* fellow in a different uniform would enter the compartment, whereupon we passengers would proffer our passports and afterwards show the pictures of ourselves to our neighbours (much laughter). Tui and I managed to snooze a little and woke just as dawn was beginning to redden the German sky. We watched the clouds over this flat, flat land grow pinker and the church spires of each town emerge in silhouette against the sunrise. It was easy to see why generations of invading hordes have used this route to march south.

Before going to the breakfast car, we welcomed a German family consisting of Poppa, two women and a teen-aged girl into the compartment. They were pretty heavy specimens all of them and as jolly as Santa Clauses. I don't think they stopped eating from the minute they got on 'til the minute they got off! They kept unpacking food from various suitcases while making gestures to us indicating how fat this was going to make them, giggling all the while. I could remember a bit of German, to my surprise, and put together sentences in my head for about half-an-hour before I dared deliver them.

Before the train pulled into Copenhagen, Tui and I ate the brown-bread sandwiches and fruit we'd brought, sitting Indian-style on our banquette. This greatly intrigued our German friends who said, *Och, das ist prima!*[1]

Tui's friend Ron met us at the station—it was about a quarter to nine in the evening—and helped us find the KFUK where we dumped our bags and then went out for a cup of coffee. I think every city should be entered first on a Sunday night. All Copenhagen was out strolling and each Dane is more beautiful than the last. We sauntered across a central square alight with neon signs in (to us) a strange language and eventually stopped at a little café where I had a glass of milk, perfectly delicious. I've been drinking Danish milk ever since.

Here, unlike Paris, no one stares at you as if you were a freak, everyone drinks it.

April 5

Yesterday we arose, took up our cameras and walked. And walked, and walked…exploring a Copenhagen which reminded me strangely of Halifax, only flatter (and cleaner)! Perhaps it was the red brick buildings with their copper roofs, just like ours. We started at the harbour, where real fishwives sell wriggling catches and the Little Mermaid gazes poetically out to sea, then on to the Royal Castle and the elegant shopping district. The little Danish girls have ribbons on their pigtails and they and their elders are so universally handsome that I began to think myself in the Land of Oz.

This is a Hans Christian Andersen anniversary (he was born in 1805) so lots of window displays are devoted to him. I got so caught up that I bought a little book of fairy stories in Danish, thus discovering that only we English speakers call him 'Hans Christian'. In Denmark he is always 'ho say' (H.C.) Andersen.

Today we took a bus tour to Elsinore, or 'the Hamlet castle' as the guide called it. I can report that Elsinore is suitably grey and misty. We also visited Frederiksborg Castle, once the royal residence, now a museum maintained by a Danish brewery. Frederiksborg smells of oak and is much more austere and simple than French or Italian castles. Everything seems to be carved out of wood—entire ceilings, for example.

For lunch (ten *kronen*) the bus stopped at a place whence one is supposed to glimpse Sweden on a clear day, (i.e. not today). There was a huge *koldt bord*[2] table. We heaped our plates. But help! The cat is out of the bag! During lunch a couple of American boys asked if Tui and I were teachers. I roared with laughter to hide the pain and told them that, in my case, they were about five months early. Tui really is a teacher, so they were half right. They hastened to explain, eyeing my slacks, that traveling teachers always seemed to be more comfortably dressed than other tourists.

An American lady on the tour confided to us, in the washroom, that she was going on to Paris. I casually said, "Oh yes, Paris. Do you know, I've been living there for six months and haven't had a bath since I arrived?" She was properly shocked whereupon I explained about the showers. Do you suppose this bit of naughtiness was a reaction to my being taken for a teacher?

April 6

We ran into a series of adventures this morning, trying to get from the KFUK to our crack-of-dawn train for the Skagerrak boat. Firstly, the front door was locked so, in order to get out, we had to squeeze our suitcases and stuff down a fire exit. Secondly, as no one was around to collect our payment for the room, we sealed it in an envelope and left it on the bedroom night table. We could have decamped without paying at all! Tui hung the key on a doorknob and we were off: boarded our train, crossed from Denmark into Sweden on the ferry, changed some money, got our passports beautifully stamped and tramped from the harbour to the railway station, all without the slightest hitch (this is NOT France). The sea was a smooth and polished grey with beautiful, glassy highlights but the crossing was frigid. I'm glad I opted for slacks to travel, even if people do look at them a bit askance.

The language about us gets more and more remote from anything 'romance'. For example, *papier* in French is *papir* in Danish and *papper* in Swedish; but coffee, train and station seem to be blissfully international terms.

Lots of hugs, Nancy Wickwiresen

[1] Hey, that's first-rate!   [2] cold buffet

on the Stockholm-to-Oslo train

Dear Parents:

Glad Påsk. That means 'Happy Easter' in Swedish and in a few hours, I'll be able to tell you what it is in Norwegian. This letter is being (very painstakingly) written on a train from Stockholm to Oslo. Don't ask me why I insist on writing while on a train. Perhaps it's the challenge, as my handwriting is bad enough anyway without the added jiggling? Furthermore we feel very glad to be on the train at all. Anyone less firm-minded than Nancy and Tui would be on their way to Uppsala right now. My dears, we have **done** Stockholm, we have **did** Stockholm, we have seen more of that city in forty-eight hours than we've seen of Paris in six months. I've never been more royally entertained—or colder—in my life.

The train got into Stockholm at 7:30 PM instead of 9:30, dear old Bennett's Travel Agency having made a slight error. Naturally my friend Sture wasn't waiting so, after a great deal of telephoning (helped by a kind Swedish man who spoke English) I made contact and Sture came right out to get us, two dirty waifs carrying a string bag full of books and oranges and a newspaper announcing Churchill's retirement.

I shall now explain about Sture Jansson and hope that the neighbours won't be scandalized. I met him last October on the Comité d'Accueil excursion to Fontainebleau and we'd exchanged a few words every once in a while since then, mostly about cameras. When he heard Tui and I were going to Stockholm at Easter, he offered to get us free beds in a Swedish flat and show us the city, as he would be back home by then. Sture inspires instant confidence, being a big, good-natured Swede, the kind you can imagine patting small kittens; so I accepted.

Anyway, Sture picked us up at the station and took us by subway to the promised flat. But, oops! When we got there we were stunned to discover that Sture and a friend, also named Sture, were living in it. The other Sture was awaiting us with a table of *smörgåsbord* and four eager guests, two of whom spoke English and two of whom did not. We looked like frights and were dead beat but hungry, too, so we sat down and had a cheese-and-fish-fest washed down with *schnapps*[1] and Swedish coffee which, after French coffee, tasted weak. The guests didn't seem shocked that we were going to sleep there, so eventually Tui and I relaxed (a bit) and before bed I even had a BATH! BATH! BATH! A lo-o-vely, long bath in a mile-long, Swedish bathtub.

The boys then made up our bed in one of the bedrooms, fussing over us like two great-uncles. We had lace-edged sheets and flowers in a vase. In the morning Sture J. knocked on the door ("What do you suppose they want?" asked Tui anxiously) and announced that he was leaving our morning tea outside. So we had breakfast in bed, like Madame la Marquise, and wished the Franco-Brit people could see us now.

That first morning we were allowed to do some shopping. Sture Hollman took us downtown in a freezing snowstorm and turned us loose with a multitude of shopping instructions and the drill for lunch, which we were to have with the two Stures. After drooling over the beautiful glass and pottery and steelware, we tramped up and down the streets in our thin nylons, shuddering every time we came to a corner and met a blast of *nordiske* wind. By noon my face was jelled and my feet moved stiffly one in front of the other. I regarded them with interest as if they didn't belong to me really. Fortunately Sture J. came charging along and got us seated at a table in the restaurant, where we thawed out rapturously.

After lunch we were shown the Opera House. As *Madame Butterfly* was playing that very evening we reserved four seats, Tui and I paying for our own after much argument.

The Stures were anxious that we should see the new housing which is Stockholm's pride and joy, so to their friend Oskar's place we went. His digs are in a huge, modern apartment block, surrounded by similar blocks. The whole complex is designed as a self-sufficient community with, in the centre, all manner of shops with marvellous Nordic names: *Frukt, Konsum, Möbler* [2] and so on. Above the shops was an ultra-contemporary restaurant, stunning enough to convert the most ardent anti-modernist and beside it, a hothouse garden with lush flowers and plants. (If it only hadn't been so COLD!)

Hospitable Oskar served us some much-needed coffee. He didn't speak English but we all got on like bugs in a rug and laughed away until it was time to catch a bus to the Opera.

We all enjoyed *Madame Butterfly*, sung in Swedish, though Tui and I could have done without a frosty, post-theatre stroll through the Old Town. We literally MELTED into bed that night.

The next day, which wasn't nearly so cold, we admired many views from many towers which we climbed and were shown the zoo and an outdoor Folk Museum. Stockholm is so clean and prosperous. All the people looked healthy and well-dressed and we didn't see a single beggar. Sture, who is a whirlwind of energy, desperately wanted us to stay an extra day in order to visit historic Uppsala. We were actually afraid he'd kidnap us in order to prevent our leaving Sweden—which is why we are so glad to be, at this minute, on the Oslo train. Another day at Sture's pace would have seen us shipped home feet first.

Photo by Sture Jansson

Sture Hollman, Nancy (frozen) and Sture Jansson in front of the Stockholm Concert Hall.

Tui and Nancy on the belfry of Stockholm's Town Hall

Mainly we couldn't get over the hospitality. When we protested against his offering us his own bed and free board, Sture J. explained that he had done a lot of hitch-hiking and people had opened their houses to him. He couldn't repay them in kind so was passing on the generosity to someone else. What a guy!

Attention, please! We've just passed the frontier and are now in Norway. Two little men—I mean, two BIG men, in uniforms, came through and stamped our passports. This is a fine, clean railway coach, all light wood and blue paint—and it's third-class. I should like to see first-class…every seat probably comes equipped with bootblack and manicurist. Outside the window are stretches of evergreens, blue sky, bare birches and snow. It could be Nova Scotia in March. Rats! No more ink in my pen. I'll finish this in the hotel.

Hotel Norge, Oslo, Norway

EASTER SUNDAY MORNING

This morning we took in the Easter service (Lutheran), visited the Folk Museum, rode up the Oslo Mountain by train, saw the famous Frogner Park with its mass of sculptures by Gustav Vigeland, looked in the shop windows and collapsed to bed, whence I write. Oslo is a nice old town but nearly deserted because everyone is off skiing.

We've found that in Norway there are only two meals a day. Breakfast was enormous, a regular buffet supper. We were so full that we couldn't manage any dinner (eaten here about 4:00 PM) except two open-face sandwiches and tea. The two-meal plan, it was explained to us, originated so that farmers and fishermen could get the most out of a short day. Much of the year it gets dark really early.

The Norwegian embroidery and pewter (*tinn*) and woolen knits are sumptuous. We shall buy in Bergen. For now, *Gode Påske*[3] and love,

Nancy

[1] A lethally strong eau-de-vie distilled from potatoes, served in tiny glasses and meant to be gulped in one draught. In 1954 it was 'rationed' to one litre per person per month.
[2] Fruit, Grocery Co-op, Furniture
[3] 'Happy Easter' in Norwegian

April 16, Hotel Emma, Rotterdam

Dear Helen:

This morning sees me sitting in the sunny breakfast room of the Hotel Emma in Rotterdam. Across from me, sipping her tea, is Tui Flower and beside me is none other than Colin Bergh, my Dalhousie classmate. As Tui and I were boarding the Bergen-to-Rotterdam boat,

Colin Bergh on board the
Bergen-to-Rotterdam steamer.

whom should I spy in the customs line ahead of us but Colin![1] He'd been visiting his Norwegian relatives and was returning via Rotterdam to Amiens and the detested *lycée*. What fun! The North Sea crossing was calm and sunny and the three of us got sunburnt faces from sitting out too long in the deck chairs.

We docked next morning, early. After the fjords everything seemed so flat! Tui and I were thankful to have Colin with us, partly to lug suitcases but mostly to speak the lingo. He found us the Hotel Emma where we took rooms, dumped our bags and rushed off to see the tulips.

It's a three-quarter hour train trip to Keukenhof, where masses of spring bulbs are planted in a lovely park landscaped with lakes and statues. The hyacinths, scillas and tulips were just opening and smelt heavenly while Wordsworthian crowds of daffodils swayed in the breeze. In the greenhouses were row upon row of named and numbered tulips, still in bloom and every one perfect. I felt quite delirious.

On the way back to Rotterdam I insisted that we stop off at Delft. Do you remember the 'familiar essay' in the Grade Eleven reader about the Delft tower? Well, we found it, sitting all clean and pure at one end of the market square and heard the many bells chime the half-hour.

We had dinner at a good, Norwegian time of day (4:30) as we hadn't eaten breakfast; and as we ate we watched an endless flood of people on bicycles riding home from work. Finally, after leaning over a canal to watch the long, long barges go through a toll gate, we went to bed.

By the way, our Bergen hotel, according to good old Bennett's, was only two minutes' walk from the Bergen-to-Rotterdam boat dock. Come Wednesday morning at 10:00 AM (we sailed at eleven) we discovered that we were, good God, two *miles* from the dock which was in the other harbour. This blooper nearly topped its predecessor, i.e. our travel schedule showed us arriving in Bergen at 7:00 PM when in fact the train doesn't pull in until midnight. By then we were so used to Bennett's bum steers that we simply giggled. And of course we did catch the boat after all.

Your ever resourceful,
Sister N.

P.S. On the Bergen wharf, Tui says, she saw fishermen bite the heads off freshly-caught herring and eat the fish raw.

[1] Colin, disenchanted with teaching, chose a career in Law. He practised alternately in Toronto and Ottawa until his death in 2004.

April 20, Collège Franco-Brit

Dear Family:

You should see Paris in April. All the leaves are out. Everywhere there are flowering trees and in the parks, forsythia and lovely rhododendron, yellow and deep rose. Everyone sits outdoors in the sun along the boul' Mich' sipping coffee and the ice-cream vendors have set up their little stalls. The grass at the Cité is covered with tiny daisies and the birds are singing as if they'd burst. I'm back!

I had a really pleasant time in Holland. Tui[1] was there one night only as she returned to Ron and Denmark so, on the second day, Colin and I took a boat tour of Rotterdam harbour, which is vast, wandered about the zoo and had supper in an Indonesian restaurant (the oddest dishes! Even Colin couldn't decipher the menu). We settled upon *rijstafel*, wheeled to us upon a wagon. It consisted of an assortment of spicy Indonesian delicacies to which one helped oneself. We decided we'd sample a bit of everything before actually heaping our plates but, as soon as we started eating, the waiter scooted over and removed the wagon (no more *rijstafel* for you!) We obviously didn't understand the protocol.

To finish off the evening we saw a film, *Désirée*,[2] starring Marlon Brando. How I giggled when Stockholm appeared on the screen, coated in snow and ice.

We had to rise at 6:00 AM the next morning to catch our train and the Emma's man promised to have our breakfasts ready in the sitting-room downstairs. This he accomplished by preparing everything the night before, so we downed stone-cold coffee amid chortles. Next we lugged our bags to the station and stepped promptly onto the wrong train. We were able to get off at Rosendal just in time to catch the right one, thank goodness. Trusty Colin rode all the way to Paris, got me safely bundled into a taxi and to the Franco I came. (I'm still chagrined over falling asleep on the train with my mouth open and drooling.)

April 21

I have in hand another letter from Peter Waite, who is arriving on the 14th of May, delegating me to reserve his hotel room and get tickets for the opera for that evening, which I shall do with immense pleasure. Hope they'll be doing *la Flûte enchantée* or *les Indes galants* even though *les Indes* is said to be in the worst possible taste. I understand they throw rose petals and waft real perfume out into the audience.

Did I tell you about the gorgeous red ski sweater bought in Bergen? I'm debating whether to get a pair of French stovepipe slacks to go with it.

French girl in slacks, rear view

Yours ever, Nancy

P.S. Dave Peel[3] has written asking if I can help him get a job here for the summer. I replied saying that (a) jobs are scarce and (b) it's not customary in France for students to have 'summer jobs' (all they do is study, it seems). However M. Lemay, if David would write to him at the Maison canadienne, might dig up some English tutoring. French parents are crazy about having their children learn English.

---

[1] Tui became food editor for New Zealand Newspapers. She married her editor-in-chief in 1980 and retired in 1984. Tui often holidays in France and no longer sneers at French cuisine.

[2] 1954 Hollywood film with Brando as Napoleon and Jean Simmons as Désirée Clary. Désirée, rejected by Bonaparte, weds marshal Bernadotte, who is elected king of Sweden.

[3] David Peel, a Dalhousie classmate, joined External Affairs (now Foreign Affairs). His postings included Ankara, Madrid, Moscow and Prague, where he served as ambassador.

Dear Mom:

This morning, oh, joy! Today, besides being another beautiful, sunny day—I'm beginning to think Paris is enchanted and will never have rain again—brought me two letters, one from you and a nostalgic one from Marc-Antoine. Dear, fragile Marc. He'd left money with one of the fellows to get me two roses, one a deep crimson and the other, the saffron-peach colour of a Parisian twilight.

This afternoon, after vocabulary class, I sauntered through the Jardin des Tuileries to l'Orangerie, walking slowly because it was so fine and warm and the pink and red tulips were out. The tourists were out, too—Paris is beginning to fill up with them and they seem to congregate around the Arc de Triomphe du Carrousel and the place de la Concorde. As a resident of Paris I feel vastly superior, though actually all I need is a camera to be taken for one myself. There's a terrific art exhibit at l'Orangerie, much better than the previous one on Van Gogh and the Auvergnat painters. This one is sponsored by the United States' *Hommage à la France* project which is mounting a series of concerts and expositions to familiarize Parisians with U.S. culture. The paintings aren't American, though, but a selection of French masterpieces from American collections. Among them are the famous, full-length portrait of Napoleon in tight white breeches, one hand inside his vest, by Delacroix, Renoir's *Rowers' Lunch*, some Toulouse-Lautrec sketches and paintings, plus Pissaros, Manets and Monets. I made the rounds while observing the other people who were there, especially the elegant Parisian women. This spring pleated skirts are high style and Parisiennes' suits **fit** properly. The current coiffures are fetching and invariably feature the few dyed or tinted tendrils which characterize the *élégante*. Add to this, beautifully polished nails and false eyelashes. Despite all the artifice, which is a bit startling, the Parisienne knows how to dress.

Afterwards I goggled into the shops on the rue St. Honoré (where the aforementioned *élégantes* order their outfits) and, since it was six o'clock, decided to wait for Monique, who works at 15, rue du

Louvre. A lounger drew nigh and hazarded, slyly, that Mademoiselle was, perhaps, awaiting him? I didn't even glance at him, knowing from experience that if I replied (*'Non, je ne vous attends pas'*),[1] he would aggressively argue the point. After a few more appeals, to which I responded by staring coldly at an iron grillwork, he stalked away, muttering, *"Vous manquez du courage."*[2]

NEWS BRIEF

Sarasu is engaged to her American boyfriend, ring and all and has invited everyone to celebrate in her room this very eve.

Love, Nancy

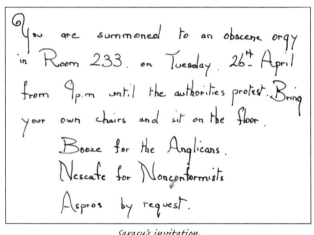

Sarasu's invitation

---

[1] No, I'm not waiting for you.
[2] "You lack courage." These invitations to romance were never-ending. We all got them—only Sarasu succumbed.

Dear Helen:

Whew! Is it hot! We're in the midst of the warmest spring Paris had had in a long time. I'm sitting at my window with the window wide open to the night air. There's *Bérénice* by Racine to read and write an essay on but I simply don't feel like doing it in such gorgeous weather, it's all I can do to keep from skipping classes. Actually, this afternoon I did skip—all the way downtown to look at the dress shops.

Darn. The *grands magasins* in Paris are so disappointing. I'd love to get a cotton frock but the only nice ones cost from 34 to 40 **dollars** while anything less expensive was in shoddy fabric with the hem sewn through to the outside, threads hanging, etc. It'd be foolish to pay so much, yet to have a 'Paris dress'....

LATER

I got my summer clothes out of the trunk to hang them up and they look nicer than anything in the stores here. Wouldn't Eaton's and Mills Brothers[1] be tickled?

Lots of love, Nancy

[1] an upscale ladies' wear store in Halifax

Author's note: Only once was I really petrified in Paris. I was trotting along the boulevard des Italiens when a 'masher' type began to tail me, chatting softly from behind but keeping pace. As usual I ignored him: but suddenly he came abreast and seized my arm while calling out loudly, in French, 'Now sweetheart, let's not quarrel', etc. as if we were in the midst of a domestic dispute. He began to drag me along the street but I wrenched away and bolted into the nearest shop, which sold yarns and embroidery equipment. The elderly vendeuse[1] slammed the door on my pursuer and bade me sit down, saying, "J'ai vu son petit jeu".[2] I waited a good twenty minutes amid the knitting needles until my heart stopped pounding and we were both sure he had gone for good. I did not dare recount this little adventure to my family.

[1] saleslady
[2] "I saw his little game."

Sunday, May 8

Dear Mom:

Being the 8th of May and Liberation Day, all Paris is decked in flags. All the collèges here at the Cité are also decked in flags; and we don't get a holiday because it's Sunday. Rats, *zût et crotte.*[1]

Yesterday morning I 'pulled myself to four pins' (as the French say) and, as the Opéra Garnier will be 'dark' on May 14, set out for the Opéra Comique to buy two tickets for *Carmen*, for Peter Waite and myself. Despite the Opéra Comique's being the most cleverly hidden building in Paris I managed to get two really good seats at 790 francs each, which I trust Peter will pay for (his famous last words were, 'and don't stint'). Actually that's only about $2.25 per seat but in francs it sounds much more. Then after lunch (asparagus, yum!) Monique and I went into town to look for a summer suit for me.

First we went to Franck & Fils where I tried on a couple of things but they were so classic and severe that I felt like a little girl dressed up in her mummy's clothes. We then went to a swishy store near the Place de l'Opéra called Maison du Blanc and quickly exited again because their suits **started** at 35 thousand francs. Back to the rue de Rivoli where we saw quite a pretty light blue suit in a window under the arcades. I tried it on. The display model they had was too big but, in Paris, all the little shops are also *couturier*² and make things up *sur mesure.*³ Best of all, the price was 20 thousand. I said, *"D'accord"*⁴ and boy, are my fingers crossed. It's to be ready on May 18. I can say, casually, that I got it 'near rue de la Paix'.

If this sounds exciting and Parisian, it is nothing compared to the day before, because the day before I trotted out to rue St. Honoré to have my hair cut and styled by Monsieur Michel at Helena Rubenstein. Michel recently cut and curled Jane Henry's hair and she looked absolutely striking. I was ushered into a carpeted and gilded hall by cool, elegant ladies in black dresses and conducted to the *premier étage* (i.e. the second floor) by a gentleman in evening clothes. There I was graciously divested of my coat and hat, given a white robe and seated in a chair before a mirror. Monsieur Michel came out and asked Madame what she desired. He studied my face, showed me several photographs of beautifully coiffed ladies, chose the most beautiful of all and began to snip away. When he had finished cutting, he proposed that I have a permanent, so, feeling reckless, I had it, thinking 'Wotthehell'. Monsieur Michel gave copious instructions to an assistante about how it was to be *gonflé* and not *frisé*,[5] whereupon I had great, heavy things clamped into my hair and was inserted under a dryer until well-done. At this point Monsieur reappeared, whipped out his comb and began to create the New Me.

Now generally speaking, the 'new' something is better than the 'old'. But if you had seen me when I hobbled out of Helena Rubenstein you'd have sworn I was the Wild Woman of Borneo. *Ah, la grande coiffure! Ah, la beauté d'une femme!*[6] Ah, phooey. I paid through the nose for it, too—five thousand francs plus a 750-franc tip. Beware, beware of hairdressers, even in Paris.

I consoled myself by humming a line from Daddy's favourite song, '♪and as for my hair, I am glad it is there, I'll feel very sad when it goes ♪', etc. Actually I shouldn't judge until I've washed and set it myself a couple of times. Stay tuned for further news.

Classes end on June 3rd. If money holds out, I want to go in May to Mont St. Michel, then see the châteaux de la Loire in June. All I need to find besides funds are a couple of girls to hitch-hike with.

There's some grammar to do so I must begin doing it.

All sorts of love from:

   and

---

[1] 'heck and turd'
[2] dressmakers
[3] made to measure
[4] O.K.
[5] wavy and not tightly curled
[6] Ah, the top-notch hairdo! Ah, womanly beauty!

11 mai

Dear Family:

Friday is the 13th and Saturday, Peter cometh. Heaven knows just when. I must find out when the plane from London lands and leave a *petit mot*[1] in his hotel room. Friday I will wash my hair for the first time since Monsieur's permanent and here's hoping Friday *le treize* won't be unlucky.

This week I've been sorting out and writing up my grammar notes so they'll be in reasonable order for the exam. It's a tedious job so I do a bit at a time while consuming quantities of Nescafé, made with milk instead of water, which is how I get my milk quota.

Mr. Marshall[2] has written saying he will consider my case as far as a teaching position at Q.E.H. is concerned but, to be eligible, I must take the summer Education course at Dal.,[3] which means I **must** sail on July 1 and forego the July 5 bourse money. Now, if I don't take the job, would it not be worth it to stay in Europe, collect my bourse, visit Maria[3] in Palermo and then sail home? What a dilemma.

Mamma, you suggested I do an M.A. Well, yes, but it would cost more money and mean more essays, more study, more exams…you've no idea what an intellectual tramp I feel at times. Piling up degrees doesn't have the lure of self-sufficiency, at least at the moment.

Last Sunday night there was a special showing of the film *French Can-can* at the Cité. If you've been following the Cannes film festival (which has currently usurped the place of Princess Margaret in our popular press), you'll have read about this magnificent colour film of Jean Renoir's, which he presented at the Festival—but didn't enter. (Faultfinders say he was afraid it wouldn't get the grand prize.) The thrill was, that Jean Renoir himself was there and addressed us afterwards. He is a plump little man, perfectly at ease and friendly

Jean Renoir addressing students after a showing of French Can-Can.

with the students, who grilled him with questions. Afterwards everyone went upstairs to the Music Room where we were served champagne and Renoir held court with crowds of students sitting at his knees. He is the son of the painter Auguste Renoir. Imagine!

Sunday afternoon I betook myself to St. Denis on the back of an open bus. There's a famous cathedral there, the first Gothic cathedral built in France; and inside it are the tombs of the French kings. It's a modest cathedral, not at all like Westminster Abbey, and the horizontal effigies are bathed in red and blue stained-glass light, quite peaceful and almost friendly.

Beth Ogilvie is going on the annual pilgrimage to Chartres this coming weekend, to the horror of Monique, who thinks only Catholics should go. Mind you, if it weren't for Peter Waite, I'd have been tempted myself. As compensation, yesterday after class I discovered a tiny, sunny park on one end of the Ile de la Cité. The Seine flowed by, the leaves were green and children played in the sand. It's going to be a wrench, come July 1.

Love n' stuff, Nancy

[1] a note

[2] Ralph Marshall, principal of Queen Elizabeth High School in Halifax.

[3] Maria married an American colleague, moved to Cleveland, had 5 children, divorced, then devoted her professional life to Early Childhood Education. Now retired, she travels, paints and is still 'just like Maria'.

May 15, noon

 Dear Family:

Duncan has come through with a letter—finally—revealing that he has for the last two weeks been articled to a law firm in Kingston, Ontario, headed by somebody named Bill Henderson, M.P. [1] He feels Upper Canada is a good choice because Halifax is really no place for yet another young lawyer.

An enthused member of the teaching profession arrived in Paris yesterday afternoon: Peter Waite. At his request we were to meet on the Pont Neuf by the statue of Henri IV (one of THE places to meet in Paris) followed by dinner and *Carmen*. It had been raining on and off all day, alternating with blue sky and fierce sun, so I was really stumped about what to wear. Finally I got out my deep blue cotton dress, the one which looks like silk. My hair calmed down nicely for the occasion and the only hitch to the whole effect was that I had to wear plastic booties over my shoes, because it was going to rain. (Parisians roar with laughter at the sight of these booties.)

I found Peter sitting by the statue, in grey flannels and a navy blazer, looking very natty. We strolled about and then went to dinner at a place nearby. O frabjous day, I no longer felt undergrad and inferior and could actually hold my own in conversation with a Dal. professor.

We had an apéritif before dinner and rosé wine with. It was great to see someone from home, especially one who fed me juicy stories about the Dalhousie senate versus the faculty. We then climbed into a cab and drove off to the Opéra Comique to see *Carmen*. I thoroughly enjoyed it, especially the good seats. Carmen herself was raven-haired and Spanish-eyed and so very vivacious that the chorus seemed wilted in comparison.

After this Peter suggested a nightcap and hitting the hay. Hm-m-m-m. I wasn't entirely sure whether he might expect the supposedly 'liberated' me to join him in the second activity—so I countered with a classic Parisian pastime, i.e. dance until dawn and then repair to les Halles [2] for some onion soup. Peter went for the plan so off we trotted to Montmartre, found a little Italian restaurant where we had some sort of spaghetti thing at the good old hour of 2:00 AM, then headed into a *Dancing* called Le Tahiti, which had good music and no tourists (except us). At 4:00 AM we took another cab down to the Seine and walked along it, looking at the lights reflected in the water and feeling a crispy, morning breeze. The next thing we knew, the sky in the east began to lighten, *camions* [3] rolled towards Châtelet to start the market and it was nearly five of the clock. Peter begged off the onion soup as he was exhausted and I don't know why I was not! Usually I feel limp as a fern after midnight, like Cinderella.

Around mid-afternoon Peter came out to the Cité bearing a large bunch of daisies, to say thank-you and goodbye, as he was off to Spain. Like so many North American intellectuals he seems to venerate everything European and tried to argue me out of returning to dull, predictable Canada. Heigh-ho! Who is right?

Maria has written a letter in which she is very cheerful about life in general. It seems little Giulio, her charge, has settled down nicely.

During the Long Weekend coming up, Elizabeth Wade and I want to explore Brittany and we plan to thumb it. We'll be a group of four girls and will travel in pairs, meeting up each evening. Everyone does this so please don't worry.

Votre tendrement dévouée, Nancy

[1] Bill Henderson became an Ontario Supreme Court judge.

[2] Les Halles was the central Paris market: established pre-12th century, improved 1850s, demolished 1971. The site is now a shopping mall (Forum des Halles) and R.E.R. hub (Châtelet). The market was moved outside Paris to Rungis.

[3] transport trucks

23 mai, midi

Dear Family:

I'm clean again. I've just had a long shower (had to soap my hair three times) and four days' accumulation of Brittany dust is gone. And the holiday was fabulous!

On a tip from experienced hitch-hikers, we traveled in pairs for safety, two Brits and two Canucks. Elizabeth (Brit) was with me and Sue Bennett (Brit) with Marjorie Holmes.[1] On Thursday the four of us set off at 8:15 of a lovely, sunny morning. I carried, for total luggage, my red shoulder bag containing a nightie, a toothbrush and toothpaste, money and passport, oh, and a bunch of travel folders and maps. We all had string bags full of hard-boiled eggs, bread and fruit for our lunches. Whee!

We took a bus to the Porte de Versailles where we separated into pairs, fixing a rendezvous at the Mère Poulard hotel in Mont St. Michel for nine o'clock that evening. Mère Poulard is a very expensive hotel but it was the only one any of us had heard of—we didn't intend to stay there. While I was in an *épicerie* buying caramels to offer the people who picked us up, Marjorie and Sue went sailing past in a Renault. Elizabeth and I were on our own.

We succeeded in stopping a big blue camion whose mustachioed driver took us half-way to Chartres. He told us proudly that he had been in the film *Si Versailles m'était contée*, produced by Sacha Guitry—as a cavalryman—in costume—and also (his trump card) he'd been in the retinue of the King of England when the latter visited France in 1937. Nowadays (sigh) he carried horses into Paris to be slaughtered.

After the horseman, we got a ride almost immediately to Chartres with a young couple. It rained off and on over the Beauce, which is a rich wheat plain all around Chartres and famous for its sudden thundershowers. The countryside is so flat that you can see the cathedral for miles—it's said to be the most beautiful in France so of course we went to visit it. Chartres cathedral has two different towers, each stunning, and the most exquisite stained-glass windows. There was a slap-up High Mass going on, it being Ascension Day, while outside women sold lace and peppermints. I cried when I saw the windows. The cathedral interior is cool and dim and so the glorious stained glass hits you as you enter.

From Chartres we hitched a ride as far as a village whose name I forget, arriving at one o'clock in the pouring rain. We found a café where one can bring one's own *manger* and opened our string bags. We did order coffee, which was prepared for us specially, in a little saucepan. After serving us, the women who ran the café settled around a fashion magazine and criticized the styles in it, just the way we do at home.

We walked out of the village and bingo! A young man in a big truck pulled up and offered to take us to Le Mans. That was a terrific distance so we jumped in and had just got nicely settled when he roared around a corner (on two wheels) into a village and pulled up. He had a rendezvous there with another truck driver and suggested that we join them 'for a drink'. **Then** he would take us to Le Mans. Elizabeth and I exchanged glances and decided to thank him very much but we'd get out on the road and try for something else. We'd had quite enough of his driving and besides, we had no idea what he meant by 'a drink'!

Alors, we headed for the road and just as it began to sprinkle again, a couple in a station wagon stopped for us. We crammed into the back seat amid piles of coats and luggage and a mongoose named Babette, in a cage. The couple were *pieds-noirs*[2] (i.e. French Algerians) holidaying in France, and were going right to Rennes. Perfect! We did note that the man's hands were covered in bites, from Babette no doubt; and soon realized that those hands belonged to a driving maniac. At times we were going so fast that Elizabeth felt ill and I just went numb. When we got to Le Mans, he headed straight for the big car racing track and hurtled around it at a terrifying speed while E. and I made little, frightened squeals. This put him in such a good mood that he bought each of us a coffee after.

As a sort of revenge, I got him to stop at Vitré to see the château. There was a lovely, late afternoon sun which mellowed everything and made the ivy on the castle shine. The streets of Vitré are tiny and twisty and the houses have been preserved intact from the Middle Ages. Each second storey protrudes over the first and is supported by wooden pillars. There is a moat on one side of the castle and a sheer, plunging cliff on the other, just like the storybooks.

From there it was just a hop to Rennes, where we were deposited outside the city on the road to Mont. St. Michel. *"Vous voyez comme je suis prudent?"*[3] he asked us, as we thanked him.

After a bit of a wait, a sweet, elderly couple picked us up and drove us to the Mont. It was a splendid, golden evening and Brittany is so wild and lovely. The couple set us down on the long road which connects the island to the mainland, saying that we, like pilgrims, should walk the last kilometer. We were as happy as fools. The sun was setting on the towers of the old abbey and all around, for miles and miles, stretched gleaming blue and amber sand flats, and above it all, the pale blue, late evening sky. A wind whistled in the grass as we tramped towards the Mont, positive that Sue and Marjorie couldn't have made it.

We inquired at the Mère Poulard but—no English or Canadian girl had come. Would we like supper at 1100 francs and a bed at 900? No, thanks. So we took about three steps further up the hill (the streets here wind around the hill like stripes around a top) and *voilà!* Hôtel de l'Espérance had a room at 600 and menu at 400 francs. We took it, washed up, ordered our meal and had just taken a sip of wine (Côtes du Rhone, the cheapest they had) and a taste of *palourde*[4] when two forms burst into the room—Sue and Marjorie! They'd been there since six-thirty, had already eaten and were sure we'd never make it.

Elizabeth and I went on with our *palourdes*, talking a mile a minute. We'd decided to have one really good meal a day, you see, with dessert and everything. The wine made us sleepy so, after a short moonlight walk up the twisty street to look out over the sea, we plopped into bed. Elizabeth said she was so full she couldn't turn over.

The next morning, full of delicious coffee and croissants, we each shelled out fifty francs and joined a party of French tourists to visit the inside of the Abbey itself, an amazing structure, built on the sheer rock. We hated to leave but had to be out of the hotel by noon. *Bon!* Off we set on foot to the mainland and Elizabeth and I got the first hitch, to Pontorson.

We found ourselves on a deserted road bordered by lush, green grass and blue, yellow and white wildflowers. We walked to the next village which grovelled in poverty—a few hens, stone huts, tired peasant women in black. Our next hitch was with a kindly gentleman who had a large water-spaniel and a bunch of asparagus in the front seat. We clambered into the back and were driven right to St. Malo, ♪*beau port de mer*♪.[5] I explained to an amazed Elizabeth that I'd learned about St. Malo before I'd ever heard of Paris. How could Jacques Cartier bear to leave this beautiful port? The sea all around is a brilliant green, which is why it's called the Emerald Coast, and the Old Town is encircled by stone ramparts. Our gentleman explained that it was bombed to bits in the war but has been authentically restored. It is simply charming—quite swanky, in fact! and has a yacht club.

We took the ferry to Dinard and started hoofing it across the Brittany peninsula to Vannes, where we were to meet the others that night. It was now six o'clock.

A woman and her little son took us out of Dinard for about five or six kilometers. The boy spoke English very well so we talked to him in our own language which pleased *Maman* very much. Next a truck driver picked us up and took us to the next village. He'd been in Montreal as a sailor, he said, and while there was royally entertained to every meal by French-Canadians.

It was by now about a quarter to seven in the evening.

The evening itself was heavenly. Pale gold and rose sky, a sweet, apple-blossom smell, birds twittering and lush wildflowers, which I twined into the meshes of my string bag as we stumped along. The poverty of the Breton people is really depressing. They live in stone hovels and keep goats. The lovely apple orchards once served to make Brittany cider but there's no demand for it anymore, so the apples go unpicked and the trees remain, taking up agricultural space and making the people poorer. Many trees had their branches pared down to the main trunks. It seems the inhabitants chop them off for firewood.

The sun got lower and redder and finally sank, shooting long, yellow rays to emphasize the shadows and darken the road. We walked and sang and walked. Our legs began to ache and we started counting the kilometer stones which border the road. Not a soul. Not a house, not a car: pitch dark. It was a quarter to nine. But the Lord has mercy on his own and at long last an automobile came along. We were carted to the next village, St. Méen-le-Grand, and deposited in front of the only hotel, two very grateful girls.

We plunged into the hotel and asked for a room but, *hélas!* three men had stopped there for the night and had taken the only three rooms. Elizabeth had a beer and I, a cider and we both looked so forlorn that the proprietor took pity on us. She led us across the road, up an alley, and climbed an old flight of stairs over a chicken roost. Lo and behold, there was a bed, covered in a vibrant fuchsia satin spread. No running water, no closet, no toilet, 150 francs. We took it and went back to the hotel for some supper. It was glorious. Soup, omelet, a lovely steak and frites, salad and a baked custard. And wine, because

Brittany water is allegedly undrinkable. Besides, the wine puts us right to sleep.

We slept amazingly well, though the bed sagged fearsomely in the middle, and awoke to the happy sounds of chickens in the morning. The little maid from the hotel, who had a solid body and thin legs like a gnome, brought us a pitcher of hot water at eight o' clock. We washed and dressed as fast as we could and crossed the road for breakfast.

Off again, walking a good distance past stumpy, armless oak trees and wretched farms. A peasant girl in rubber boots drove a herd of cows across the road in front of us and we could see, through the trees, peasant women in black kerchiefs, knitting and watching their cows.

A man, his wife and their little girl came along just then and offered to take up to Lorient. We hadn't planned on Lorient but accepted—anything to get off that lonely road. We arrived about noon, thanked the couple and set out to look for a restaurant with a sign *ici on apporte son manger*[6]...and a toilet. We decided we wanted soup and knew we'd have a battle, because French people have a fixed idea that soup is only served in the evening. We finally found a bistro where they served us a big pot of cabbage and carrot soup for 50 francs each.

Once out of Lorient, we flagged an elderly gentleman in an enormous new Versailles automobile, which corresponds to a Cadillac. He took us around the shore so we could see his beloved Breton coast; explained about the Breton language and costumes; and left us finally at Concarneau.

Concarneau is a truly picturesque fishing village with an old walled town and a pretty little harbour. Lots of the old women here, as well as in Lorient, wore the traditional Breton lace caps, long, black skirts, black stockings and had their hair skinned back. The all looked about age 80...worn, wrinkled and shapeless...and darned if they weren't wheeling wheelbarrows and riding motor-bikes! They looked most disapprovingly at us because we were in slacks.

From Concarneau we got easily to Quimper by 5:50 PM, took a room in the Hôtel Moderne (which of course was anything but) and went off to see the cathedral. It's the one on the 12-franc stamp and it's lovely if a bit fussy.

The next morning we ordered breakfast in bed, just for fun, and then hit the road for Carnac. It was a beautiful, sunny day, the fields were thick with deep red clover, daisies, buttercups, tiny scarlet pimpernels and blue flowers. (At last I know what a pimpernel looks like! I so love Baroness Orczy's book.)[7] We got to Carnac about noon and had a devil of a time trying to find the prehistoric stones. They stand unmarked and deserted, sweeping back in long, mysterious rows over a dry, whistling plain. It was silent and eerie.

We sat down in the middle of it all and ate our lunch of bread and cheese and apples, feeling very Stone Age. Then we planted ourselves on the road to Vannes and we waited.

Nancy at Carnac

And we waited,
 and waited,
  and waited…..

…a couple of little children approached and asked, in unison, if we wanted to hear the legend of the stones. We said "*Allez-y*" and they reeled off yards of saga, chanted in a schoolroom sing-song. The little boy kept forgetting but his sister plugged doggedly through to the end. We gave them some chocolate and five francs each and they went off to play tags among the menhirs (the correct name, apparently, for the stones).

Finally a man and his great-great-great-great grandfather took us to Auray, not before we'd refused a Knight Errant on a motorcycle who offered to take ONE of us. Nope.

At Auray we had the most tremendous luck of all. A travelling businessman picked us up and remarked casually that he was headed for Paris. "*Uh...nous allons à Paris, nous aussi...*" Elizabeth said, hesitantly. He was willing to take us. Hooray!

And so we went whirling along the Loire, through Angers, had supper at Le Mans and reached Paris by midnight. The man, who was a really good egg, drove us right to the Cité gates. And withal, we were home before the 1:30 AM curfew. (Marjorie and Sue didn't get back until 4:30 AM.)

And now my story is done. It was the most wonderful vacation I've ever spent in my life. Elizabeth and I got on splendidly—neither of us complained about anything and minor hardships such as aching feet and chicken roost beds were all part of the fun. I've decided that a four-day hitchhiking trip should be an essential pre-requisite to a betrothal of marriage.

Now, I'm planning to go to Avignon on the coming weekend as we students have a Monday holiday. Virginia Johnson and I have arranged to be (illegal) passengers in a camion. We'll pay the *camionneur* 2500 francs each, which is less than half the train fare.

Then I've GOT to buckle down to some grammar as exams begin the third of June.

Love, Nancy

[1] Marjorie, from North Bay, Ontario, was also a bursary winner. She married Don Bowman and taught French until her husband finished his Law degree. Don later became a judge of the Federal Tax Court.

[2] Originally a nickname for barefoot Algerian bargemen, *pied-noir* eventually included the French landowners as well.

[3] "See how cautious I am?"

[4] clams

[5] ♪*A St. Malo, beau port de mer*♪ is a loved Quebec folksong

[6] Here you may bring your own food

[7] *The Scarlet Pimpernel*, set during the French Revolution

May 27, morning

Dear Mom:

Virginia and I are off to Avignon at two o'clock this afternoon—our *camionneur* is scheduled to leave les Halles between two and three. There are so many things to see. I'm loaded with maps and folders. Roman ruins everywhere—the Pope's palace—and several Pentecôte festivals.

Guess what? We were so enthusiastic about Brittany that a chain reaction has been set off. Two more groups are heading there this weekend.

Peter Waite has been mailing me enraptured, poetic letters describing the different cathedrals he's visited in Spain. I'm sending the Spanish stamps to Mr. Slaughter[1] who has started a collection.

Adios, amigos! Nancita

---

[1] The Rev. Norman Slaughter was the Minister at St. Matthew's United Church in Halifax. Two years later he would conduct Duncan's and my marriage ceremony.

May 31, afternoon

Dear Family:

I address you once again with wet hair, having got back this morning at 5:00 AM, grimy but happy, from Provence. Here is my tale.

Virginia and I left the Cité at noon on Friday and met our lorry drivers at les Halles. They had thick Midi accents both of them, i.e. they pronounced all the 'e's at the ends of words. One was named Charles, pronounced Charl-eh; the other's name we never discovered. Off we tooted, riding all four in the high, front seat of the most immense *poids-lourd*[1] in France, filled with fifteen tonnes of corrugated iron roofing. Charl-eh and his Second were going to take turns driving and the Spare would sleep in a little sort of berth behind the front seat, concealed by a black pull-curtain.

The boys sat on the left, with me in the middle and Virginia on the far right. After the first half-hour I realized that this trip was going to be hard on my throat as *les gars* were gabby and my French plus their accents and the thundering roar of the truck made screaming necessary. Ginny sat smugly in her corner not having to say a word.

France flattens out below Paris in a continuation of the Beauce plain, except on the east, the plain is called la Brie and that's where they make Brie cheese. There were black and white cows everywhere.

About seven o'clock we were rolling peacefully along the Yonne river in Bourgogne when boom!! a flat tire. The two fellows fussed and fumed, called the truck *pourri*[2] and a lot of other things and, when they'd finished cursing, fished out tools and a spare. Virginia and I took advantage of the break to answer a call of nature and also admire the Yonne and the fields between it and the road. Wandering about knee-deep in grass and wildflowers, I picked vermilion poppies, brilliant pink clover (not wine-red as in Brittany), buttercups and several purple-y flowers I'd not seen before.

The tire fixed, we all got in again. Since Charl-eh had to be in Marseille the next evening we were going to travel non-stop and eat our suppers on the move. We munched our way through town after Burgundian town while the chaps peeled bananas and tossed the skins out the window. We were always in sight of the river, the setting sun and a flushed sky.

If the afternoon had been fun, night was hellish. The seats got uncomfortable, we were tired and dirty, I got a crick in my back which would NOT go away and Virginia got her period. We'd nod off fitfully only to wake again and stare benumbed at the black road ahead of us.

It was dawn when we got to Lyon and just outside the city we stopped, oh bliss! for coffee. The café was full of truck drivers many of whom were restoring themselves with little glasses of *marc* (a really potent sort of brandy). Here we were told that the inspectors from Lyon southward were very strict about illegal passengers, so we'd both have to squish into the bunk behind the little black curtain. Now imagine the two of us in a space the size of a camp cot, me with my feet under V.'s nose and vice versa, our forms hidden under a smelly, green coverlet. We were both so drowsy that this seemed the summit of luxury and we dropped off to sleep immediately.

At Avignon we were set free, right beside the famous *Pont d'* of the song, at around noon of a lovely day. We paid the camionneurs their 2500 francs apiece and breathed a sigh of relief as they rumbled away. We were ravenous, so we bought some cheese and fruit and spread a picnic lunch under the Pont, just outside the ramparts. Here the Rhône is bordered with sand grass so it was almost like a seaside picnic.

Then we inspected the Papal Palace, which is incorporated into the city wall, while its gardens overlook the Rhône and another (ruined) castle on the opposite bank, built by Philippe le Bel to keep an eye on his captive, the Pope. The palace interior, saith the guidebook, was stripped by Napoleon, who had it transformed into army headquarters—so today there is nothing to see but bare walls. The gardens are much more impressive. There is a lovely, shadowy grotto with roses and swans, beautiful trees and a cool, dark fountain. Ginny had cramps and was feeling crummy so we had a cup of tea, rested and decided to push on to the Pont du Gard,[3] there to stay the night.

As Virginia wasn't up to hitch-hiking we took a bus and what a lark! Jam-full of hot, smelly natives of the region, few of whom were hotter or smellier than we. Everyone was friendly and talkative. The countryside is as different from Brittany as can be. Tall, black cypresses, vineyards, houses with red clay 'flower-pot' roofs and the famous cherry orchards, loaded with fruit. Other orchards of twisted olive trees, all silvery, surrounded tiny, ancient towns, each nestled about its church.

The bus driver dropped us about two kilometers from the Pont du Gard and we strolled the rest of the way, picking flowers and admiring the massive Roman aqueduct. Ever since seeing a picture of it in my Latin grammar book I've longed to come here.

le Pont du Gard

There was a hotel right below the Pont called Le Vieux Moulin, which had a patio and vines, big terra-cotta jars and a room for 700 francs. Sold! There were no other tourists nor inns that we could see, only the river, the trees and the aqueduct. Before supper we ran down a vine-covered path to the Gardon river and gazed at the Pont and at its reflection, all yellow in the water below. Ginny skipped stones and I took off my shoes and socks and waded a bit. We could see a camp site on the other side of the river: yellow tents and French voices through the trees. French people adore *le camping*.

After dinner Virginia collapsed to bed and I walked—or rather, inched—across the aqueduct, fingers crossed (there are no guard rails). A family of French picnickers was having supper under the first arch, lighted by a flashlight. The children thought it the hugest fun in the world.

The next morning dawned blue and blond and hot. I woke first (as usual) and went to sit on the stone terrace. The aqueduct loomed across the river, even yellower now in the morning sun—and on the opposite bank, an old man and woman were busy burning coffee beans in a smoky black stove. I sniffed for the lovely coffee smell but there wasn't any.

We set off hitch-hiking for Nîmes at mid-morning and thumbed a drive with a youngish couple. She was *de Paris*, she wanted us to know, while he was *du pays*[4] and keen on bullfights. Surely we were

going to see the special Pentecôte *mise-à-mort* at Nîmes? As neither of us had ever seen a bullfight, we decided to go.

The old Roman arena

Well! The bullfights take place in the old, Roman *arènes* which look like a mini-Colosseum. We bought the cheapest possible tickets and climbed 'way up to sit on the topmost stone seats—seats which have been sat upon for two thousand years. It was hot, so we put scarves on our heads and watched the arena fill up. Everyone was gaily dressed in pinks, yellows, scarlets and blues.

Finally the trump sounded.

The doors opened.

Enter: two black, Renaissance-clad figures on horseback, their costumes enhanced by white collars and plumed hats. The band played the bullfight music from *Carmen*. The horses did fancy steps up and down the arena.

Enter on foot: Monsieur le Toréador and Messieurs les Matadors, in gorgeous, pale blue spangled costumes with dazzling green, purple and pink satin capes, black velvet berets, knee socks and sashes.

Enter: Messieurs les Picadors, on horseback, in equally gorgeous costume. All this assembly paraded from one side of the arena to the other, bowing and scraping to the audience.

Enter finally: two clumping, big brown horses, dressed in plumes and ribbons.

Next, the whole cavalcade exited except for the toreador and the matadors, who took off their gorgeous capes and donned simpler red and yellow ones. Then…

ENTER THE BULL!

He was a poor, tired, black bull with a pique stuck in his back, two ribbons hanging from it. He didn't snort or paw the ground and I thought of Ferdinand in my storybook, the little bull who preferred to smell the flowers.

There was a lot of fancy horseplay as the matadors shook their capes and the bull came rushing towards them. The picadors came prancing along next and stuck the poor beast full of piques. The matadors added still more, all in such gorgeous colours that the bull began to look like a Christmas-tree ornament. By this time he was bleeding pretty badly and obviously weak. Our hero the toreador (named Antonete) fussed about a bit with his cape and finally, with a noble gesture, thrust a sword into the bull's heart—only he made a mistake and punctured the lungs instead and the poor beast spat out streams of blood and must have suffered terribly before he died.

When the bull was *bien mort* the two brown horses we'd seen earlier were led in and they dragged him out. Virginia and I also went out. Ugh!!

We slept that night at Beaucaire, where we found the Hôtel Napoléon: one double bed, 500 francs. The bed protested loudly at every turn and I expected a spring to pop up in the middle of my back with a twang-g-g.

The next morning, our last day, Virginia wanted to see les Baux-de-Provence, an incredible, deserted village built right into the rock. As I was asking the hotel manager about it a couple overheard me and offered to drive us out, provided we agreed to visit the château at Tarascon first. Of course we did! And it's a beautifully preserved, mediaeval castle with huge fireplaces, a moat and little turrets on the roof.

At Tarascon (*hélas!*) their car broke down just as it began to sprinkle. They apologized profusely but advised us to try hitch-hiking. No dice. Every car was full of either Grandma and Grandpa or camping equipment. We did get as far as St. Rémy, admired les Antiques (erected to the glory of Augustus Caesar in about A.D. 30), saw the madhouse where Van Gogh was interned and the newly-excavated Roman village of Glanum; but we could NOT get to les Baux. And we were getting soaked with rain. So, admitting defeat, we got a bus back to Avignon, purchased third-class train tickets back to Paris and some picnic fodder and boarded the train at 6:00 PM. We spread a napkin on the seat, hauled out a bottle of wine and, except for lack of candles, had ourselves a stylish supper.

Paris at four-thirty in the morning may be inspiring to poets but we felt, and looked, like the dirty old vagrants—called clochards—who sleep under the bridges, lacking only a broken-down baby buggy full of our tattered belongings to resemble them exactly. *Ah, la vie!* I slept until noon. *Ah, le lit!*

The poor old clochards slept on the walkways which run under each bridge.

As a trip it wasn't on a par with Brittany but then, what could be? Virginia and I kept our tempers and we've seen Provence.

I also made a decision. This afternoon I collected my June *bourse* money and bought a boat ticket to Québec. It cost 59,000 francs, which gives me enough over to pay for the train to Le Havre plus the expense of shipping my trunk. I felt suddenly, strangely happy to have The Ticket in my hand. Whoopee! I'm coming home!

First, though, I must study some grammar. The exam is on Friday.

Love, Mademoiselle-from-Avignon

[1] heavy transport

[2] rotten

[3] The aqueduct was constructed by the emperor Claudius in 1 AD, to bring water to Nimes.

[4] a local chap

June 5, Sunday

 Dear Mom:

Marjorie Holmes, the Canadian girl who went with us to Brittany, left this morning for Le Havre and the boat back to Canada—so—last night a bunch of us treated her to dinner at a little place called Le Parthenon. We all ordered roast chicken and ice cream with strawberries and afterwards, we wandered along the Seine. The sky was grey in the east but pale blue and pink in the west, barred in deep, indigo clouds. The river was a deep, stained-glass blue and the bridge lights reflected in it were quick-gold and shimmery red. How perfect for Marjorie's last evening! While we were ambling along, Sue Bennett (who, I must explain, is fair-haired, plump and very pretty) gave a startled little shriek. A young man had run up, put his arms around her, kissed her cheek and then scampered away. How we giggled! Sort of a Georgie Porgie *français*.

I wrote the grammar exam on Friday morning and, as usual, ran out of time and practically scribbled down my verbs in the subjunctive while Madame Teyssier went about snatching papers off desks.

TUESDAY

Here I sit in my window, smelling the good rain smell and watching the gentle drops roll off the leaves. The grass is five shades greener than it was yesterday and it's covered in tiny daisies.

I had my grammar oral exam yesterday afternoon (Mme Stourdzé told me I had done *très bien* on the written paper). The worst part of the oral was the waiting. I was scheduled for 4:15 PM and like a fool, arrived at 4:15 PM, thinking that perhaps just this once things would be run off smoothly? *Jamais.* I was tested at a quarter past six. Never mind—I'm in France. The day after tomorrow I'll sit the composition exam.

Oh! I forgot to tell you—Sunday evening I donned my flouncy taffeta cocktail dress and trotted off to Le Crazy Horse (a hot-spot night club on the avenue George V), as Nouhé's guest. We entered a street door and descended to the *cave*, which is done up in pseudo-Wild West style. It was very crowded, dark and intimate. The show was a hoot, mostly strip-tease, which I'd never seen before in my life. One of the strippers was billed as *la belle Canadienne* and to prove it, she came wiggling out in a leopard-skin get-up. *Ah, Paree!* There were other acts: mimes, jugglers and a male vocal trio. Quite the antidote to exams, yes? Most of the audience was American but there were lots of French people too.

Ces adorables Kira TeRiToF, Elaine DANA MiSS CANDiDA "La Reine du Strip-Tease", Rita Cadillac, LiLi LAPUDEVR ainsi que CHA LONDRES (corde) et Valerie LAFRYTH (cheval d'argon !..) se produisent chaque soir au .... CRAZY HORSE SALOON en chair et en os (si peu) et se strip-teasent intégralement ..yes... pour la joie de vos yeux – Ces ravissantes sont entourées de REPP le bafouilleur, des ... ROSSiGNoLS siffleurs, du " Zodiaque " et du mime burlesque " JuLieN "

au CRAZY HORSE SALOON dès 22h 30 sweet music à 23h 30 Show AU BAR et promenoir visibilité ToTale DRINKS depuis 500 frs. Dans la Salle le 1er Verre 1250 frs. renouvellement 400. ce qui vs permet de rentrer ivre-mort sans pour autant ruiner votre épouse.
* Evidemment champagne non obligatoire
* * A visiter les waters là-place.
* * * La cigarette-girl ne saurait vendre que cigarettes et ne pourrait vous fournir ni bas NYLON, ni chocolat ni boutonnière.
* * * * S'il vous arrive de régler votre note avant de nous quitter faites le à votre convenance, en dollars, livres, marks, roubles, Travellers, Nous vous donnerons le change "du jour" et n'exigeons aucune carte d'identité aux porteurs de chèques bancaires, vous Nous faîtes confiance NOUS VOUS FAISONS CONFIANCE AUSSi
CRAZY HORSE SALOON 12 AV. George I
PARiS 8e BAL. 6969

Le Crazy Horse opened in 1951, a cabaret where le striptease *had been elevated to state-of-the-art perfection. In its heyday it welcomed the cream of* le tout Paris. *As the decades wore on, however, it became 'old-fashioned'. Utterly depressed, the founder, Alain Bernardin, shot himself through the heart in 1994.*

THURSDAY

My composition exam this morning was no picnic. Here is the subject: '*Harmony and diversity. In your opinion, can this formula be applied to French literature? Give your reason by means of an examination of the literary works which we have studied in class.*' Another oral, my last exam, is next week.

There's to be a big, whoopee, Farewell cocktail party at the Comité d'Accueil tomorrow evening from 5:30 to 7:30, after which Jane Henry and Jean Logsden are hosting their own farewell punch party at the Maison canadienne, from nine o'clock 'til midnight. I'm to help by buying fruit and *petits fours* and stirring the punch. One by one we are leaving Paris to get on with our real lives.

Veuillez agréer, mes très chers amis, l'expression de ma dévotion la plus sincère.

Nancy Brown Wickwire, B.A.

Dear Mother:

We've had a great shock today at the Collège Franco-Britannique. Lame Peter, whose last name I don't know, is dead. Dead! He died in the métro this morning—I think he slipped on a step. Just like that; as simple a thing as that! Peter is—was—a cheerful, handsome boy with a North of England accent who always said '**egg-zam**' for 'exam'. He had a cane and one built-up shoe; but he could hop down those métro steps two at a time like anyone else, to catch a train. He always wore a navy blazer and grey flannels and went regularly to classes at the British Institute, groaning and moaning and joking about grammar and phonetics and the crowded métro, just like the rest of us. He was devoutly Catholic and went regularly to Mass every Sunday. For the first time in weeks I ate breakfast downstairs this morning and saw him there…I remember meeting him near the Sorbonne one day last week and we kidded about classes and **egg-zams**. I'd had two exams already and he was headed to his last class of the year. I remember thinking, 'I must really begin carrying my address book around with me, for I'll be seeing people whom I may not meet again before the end of June'.

We're a colony of young, energetic people here at the Cité and Death doesn't enter into our calculations at all. If one of us dies, it is like a great, mysterious snatching. There is no answer to 'Why?' It just IS, period. We say, 'It's a terrible thing, awful, yes, simply dreadful' and go on ironing our blouses in the laundry room, having thrown a sop of adjectives at Death—whom we supposed so far, far, far away from us.

There was an accident at Le Mans this past weekend during the car race. One of the vehicles exploded and killed, decapitated, maimed or otherwise injured 85 people. And we said, 'How-dreadful-it's-simply-terrible' without much emotion because we know that it won't prevent a recurrence. People will continue to race cars, others

Where to Find It

The Globe and Mail

Showers, Cool
High Here 65

112th Year. No. 32,917.　　*Final Edition*　　TORONTO MONDAY, JUNE 13, 1955.　　5 Cents Per Copy　　42 PAGES

Disaster at Le Mans

RACE CAR KILLS 78

Flying Parts Rip Through Dense Crowd

By ARTHUR O. SULZBERGER
New York Times Service

Le Mans, France, June 12. — The death count in what is believed to be the world's worst automobile racing accident climbed to 78 today. Of 77 other victims still in hospital, eight were in grave danger.

The shock of the tragedy completely overshadowed the victory of Mike Hawthorn of Britain, driving a Jaguar, which ended the 24-hour Le Mans race here this afternoon.

The watchers were quiet compared to the jammed masses who crowded, sometimes 20 to 30 deep, yesterday afternoon along the four-feet earth barrier surrounding the course.

It was into such a jam that the motor and wheels of a Mercedes, driven by Pierre Levegh, a Frenchman, tore their bloody way, ripping, cutting, mashing and burning everything in their way. It was the density of the crowd, standing along a stretch where there was no grandstands, that made the accident so massively lethal.

The whole car appeared to flip and spin into the crowd, where it seemed to explode. In reality,

The Le Mans disaster made world headlines.

Like Battlefield After Shell Burst Is Scene of Death and Havoc at Le Mans
Smoke rises from car which seemed to explode as it hurtled into group of spectators of 24-hour endurance race.

will go to watch them and gory, accidental deaths simply add to the piquancy of things. But Lame Peter's death is too close. It's odd but he now seems to us almost, well, holy, because he is somewhere, or something, which none of us can grasp. Or, is he nowhere and nothing? I'm talking about him so he isn't yet 'nothing'. Is it that we refuse, egotistically, to accept that Glorious Man can dissolve into nothingness? And therefore write poems and erect tombstones to prove that the dead live still?

I spent the weekend at Fontainebleau with Monique's family and it was very, very pleasant. Monique lives in a nice house on a nice street and all the houses are enclosed by fences. Her parents were extra kind and spoke French ver-r-y clearly and slo-o-owly at first 'til they found I really could keep up.

On Sunday, after the family returned from early Mass (I stayed blissfully in bed) we had chocolate and real TOAST for breakfast. As it was raining, M. Artiguebieille offered to take us in his *quatre chevaux*[1] to see the town and district. We drove through the lovely, green Forêt de Fontainebleau to a picturesque little town called Moret. There were fishermen all along the river, a favourite Sunday pastime in France. It became evident that M. Artiguebieille's real goal was to show me their new house which he is having built on the outskirts of Fontainebleau. As we drove along, our attention was drawn to the various roofs, doors, etc., on other houses, for comparison purposes, exactly the way we did when our Halifax house was being built.

Le déjeuner was at one-o'clock and so help me, it lasted three and a half hours. It began with apéritifs and salted 'bites', then an hors d'oeuvre of tomatoes, then salami with butter, then a sort of pastry shell filled with mushrooms in pink sauce, then roast chicken, then a platter of mixed vegetables, then a tray of cheeses, then coffee, then chocolates (which I had brought for Madame A.), then liqueurs. I had to eat everything because Madame had prepared it specially but, what with all that—and two kinds of wine—I was sleepy and my tummy, not used to big meals any more, HURT. We all did the dishes while Madame A. and I discussed refrigerators and stoves and how to make coffee.

I didn't want any dinner but on it came at eight o'clock. Again apéritifs and 'bites', cream soup, ham, cauliflower, salad, cheese, crème caramel, cake and coffee. Ouf! We all knew each other much better by dinnertime and were joking and making fun of ourselves. The stiffness was gone. Madame A. must have liked me because she invited me back for another weekend, which is immensely flattering because French people are notoriously inhospitable to strangers.

My last exam is Thursday at 2:15 PM. It's the dreaded oral and I'm the first poor devil to go in. They've reversed the alphabetical order. For once at least I won't have to wait.

Love to all, Nancy

---

[1] four horsepower automobile

Chère Maman:

This is the last letter you need answer because the Samaria, with me aboard, is expected to dock in Québec City on Saturday, July 9. I'll get the Ocean Limited to Halifax that very night and thank you, Daddy, for offering to make the train reservation.

At last the exams are over and I'm FREE. Yesterday's was the last one, an oral *explication de texte*.[1] I drew number 13, if you please, which turned out to be a passage from *Madame Bovary*. I found the passage hard to explicate without repeating myself over and over again. At the end the examiner said *"Pas mal"*,[2] which is probably a pass but definitely not honours. Huh.

Afterwards I had a rendezvous with Nicole Pouzargues. Having no definite plan, we decided, on a whim, to climb to the top of Notre-Dame Cathedral. Up we started. After about two minutes we remembered that it was Thursday afternoon, the weekday half-holiday for children in France. Every schoolmistress had her class there on an excursion and as we wound our way up the narrow, spiral staircase, long corkscrews of little boys were scrambling down, counting vigorously, *"...cent et un, cent deux, cent trois..."*

The first platform provides a fine view of the square below and of the hideous gargoyles which sit in odd corners, munching human bodies or else shooting straight out from the cathedral wall as waterspouts. Expecting to meet the ghost of the Hunchback of Notre-Dame, we visited the great bell, which is over three centuries old and can be heard at a distance of ten kilometres. We then climbed right up to the top of the cathedral and had a splendid view over Paris. It was slightly hazy, hence, perfect, as Paris rarely has a shining clean, blue sky. Those postcard shots of the Arc de Triomphe and the Tour Eiffel against a deep, sapphire background are *trompeuses*.[3] To complete our mediaeval day, we rode the métro to Vincennes to see the old fortress, a most forbidding structure.[4] It's now a museum.

I've met a Canadian boy from Québec City named Jacques. He's an engineer, has been on special education leave in Germany all year and stopped in Paris on his way back home. He's with another French-Canadian named, oddly enough, Fraser! Fraser and Jacques are here for a few days only (in fact, the pair of them are going to Spain tomorrow). Gosh, I'm so very, very proud to be able to converse easily with my fellow Canadiens in their own language. I get more thrill out of that than of any Sorbonne diploma. Interestingly, the two boys find Paris a let-down and Parisians less than charming. Their accents are mocked and the glorious *Mère Patrie*,[5] to their surprise, is full of unhelpful citizens. Jacques became poetic in his description of the North American breakfast, starting with orange juice. The other afternoon, Jacques asked if there was any part of Paris I hadn't 'done', for he certainly hadn't seen any of it. Well, except for nightclubs, I hadn't 'done' Montmartre; so we went to the Sacré-Coeur, had coffee at the Place du Tertre, gawked at the busloads of beautifully-dressed American tourists and just talked. Having both been students all year, we compared experiences and I have concluded that I definitely got the better deal.

I haven't 'done' the châteaux de la Loire either, so, Beth Ogilvie and I are hitching down to Blois on Monday afternoon, visiting the

Monique and Nancy behind the Franco-Brit.

Nancy and Nicole at Vincennes.

châteaux Tuesday and Wednesday and coming back Wednesday night. Yippee! I'd have felt so disappointed to have left France without seeing them. Then there'll be washing and ironing, getting my hair cut, packing and paying for the truck to cart my trunk and giving 'farewell' after-dinner coffee parties.

I've already washed three sweaters and am in the process of getting my two others dirty enough to wash. Methinks I'll need the seven days' rest on the boat.

Your ever faithful, N.B.W.

[1] interpretation of a text

[2] 'Not bad'

[3] faked

[4] 14th century fortress. Henry V of England died here of a sickness in 1422.

[5] Mother Country

Tuesday, June 21

 Dear Family:

Remember my lovely visit with Monique's [1] family in Fontainebleau? Well, I went again last weekend and it was such fun. We all went walking on Saturday evening in the famous Fôret and then, on Sunday, nine of us packed into two cars (the *quatre chevaux* and the larger company car at M. Artiguebieille's disposal) and drove through it, stopping to climb over rocks and look at views.

Madame Galopin, their neighbour, came for supper and Pierre-the-boarder was invited to stay as well so we had a full table. Madame Galopin interrogated me on my Canadian *habitudes* and customs—and drew back in horror when I revealed that, at home, we drink milk with every meal. 'Even with roast beef? Even (conjuring up the ultimate sacrilege) with CHERRIES?' I replied, "*Mais oui, Madame,*" and laughed, because it's the kind of question I've been asked all year. French people just don't believe it's possible.

This time the meal lasted only an hour, there weren't so many courses nor so much ceremony, so I wasn't a bit uncomfortable. I'd brought some *petits fours* as a house present. A French petit four is not a baking-powder cake cut into cubes and iced with shiny pink frosting, it's just a cookie. The whole 300 grams were eaten at a sitting.

Today I must take my *feuille d'attestation* [2] for the professor to sign and then prepare for the Loire trip. Beth and I are leaving at two-thirty this afternoon.

Love and kisses, Nancy

[1] Monique married a childhood friend, Bernard Gonssard. The couple moved to Provence where together they operated a construction company before retiring to the Marseille area. We still write and visit.
[2] certificate of accreditation

June 25

Dear Family:

What is so rare as a day in...(one guess)? Out here behind the Franco the sun is shining, a little breeze prevents it from being too hot, the birds are twittering madly though it's exactly midday; and I pause from my labour to rest and write a letter. And I mean labour, too...I went out this morning, bought a box of OMO [1] and have been washing pajamas and towels and socks ever since. Going somewhere is so complicated when you have to pack up lock, stock and barrel. I've been mailing little parcels to myself addressed to N. Wickwire, Halifax—this to reduce the agony of trying to pack everything into my trunk. If numerous brown-paper packages flow in 'to Nancy from Nancy', they're not stolen Russian icons, just old papers and books. Russian icons, by the way, are hot black market items and it seems students are the ideal couriers.

I'm going to Nicole Pouzargue's this afternoon for tea and to see the famous rose gardens at L'Hay-les-Roses. This evening there's a reception given by our school and—Oh! Oh! Oh! I forgot to tell you!

JE SUIS REÇUE!

...which means, in English, that I am 'received'; in other words, I have passed my Groupe 1, *français littéraire* exams and the *culture classique* exams and am in line for a magnificent certificate. And passing isn't automatic, either—some kids who have been in Groupe 1 since last September have flunked. Behold, I am now a cultivated woman (*une femme cultivée*, as the French say).

Get ready for the saga of the Loire valley trip.

Beth and I started out on Monday afternoon at about four-thirty, leaving from the Porte d'Orléans and, hooray, got as far as Orléans that night. The weather was glorious though I'm getting a little tired of travelling through the Beauce. Our last hitch was with a burly fellow who was carrying what looked like the components of a pre-fabricated apartment block on a trailer hitched to his car, hence he dragged along so-o-o-o slowly, me sitting on Beth's knee as the frames overflowed into the front seat. At Orléans we made for an Auberge de Jeunesse, which only charges 80 francs a night for students and members. When the manageress asked for our *pièces d'identification*, Beth realized with horror that she'd come away with neither her passport nor her student card. Now to be without any identity papers, in France, is the most criminal of crimes, as you will understand when I show you the twenty-odd cards I need just to breathe here. Madame, in the fullness of her might, berated Beth for a humiliating five minutes before refusing us a bed. Well. Now what?

The first hotel we tried had no free rooms but the *patronne* took pity on us and phoned another establishment to see if they had space. We could hear a mounting argument *en français* from the telephone booth. 'No, Madame, these are not tramps. I don't send you that sort of customers. They're two nice, young girls. NO, Madame. I'm a good judge of character. I know when I see a person what sort they are and I tell you, these are (whispering) What nationality are you? ME: *Je suis Canadienne*... these are two little Canadians, so there! What more do you want? Fine. Yes, Madame. Thank you.'

It's nice to have such a useful and well-liked nationality.

The next morning we visited the cathedral and a charming, sixteenth century mansion which are about all that's left of the old Orléans after the bombardments, then started along the Loire road, hitching towards Blois. Our first lift was with two American G.I.'s, on leave from their post in a nearby military hospital. There are lots of G.I.'s stationed at Orléans, where their presence is most unwelcome. These two were friendly and so naïve because they didn't begin to guess how much the French resent them. They don't even speak French. They took us miles out of their way just in order to have someone to speak to in English. Surely if they'd try to integrate themselves more with the French, learn the language, etcetera, it would be better for both sides? The two Yanks took us a long way past rich, green fields, worked by black-clad peasant women in long skirts and aprons; past men in the traditional peasants' smocks and wide cummerbunds; past hay-wagons and hand-picking; past acres of wheat, of oats, of beets, of clover and poppies.

They dropped us beside a little château we'd never heard of, called Ménars. (Quick, the guide-book.) Ménars is a true Renaissance castle which looks down, smiling, upon the Loire. We were the only visitors. Planted in tubs before the entrance were little orange trees, one in bloom. What a heavenly scent, quite intoxicating! The others had little green oranges growing on them. Behind the château is the rose garden, overlooking the river. Such roses! Masses of deep-red globes of perfume…and now and then, a salmon-coloured or yellow rose tree. Against the white of the castle, in the morning sun, it was breathtaking.

We reached Blois by noon, starving. The château there is a real fortress which, at one point, was delivered by Joan of Arc. It has a marvellous, circular staircase in the courtyard called *L'escalier de François Ier*,[2] on which horses could prance up and down. The town itself is quaint but quite touristy as it's a centre for tourist excursions.

From Blois, and after our picnic lunch beside the Loire (alas, rather smelly just along here, phew, phew) we were picked up by a delightful little *curé* and his dog, who took us as far as Chaumont and flattered me no end by saying that the Loire valley had nothing on the St. Lawrence river valley. In my view, they're equally beautiful.

At Chaumont we could see the château clearly as its white towers soared above the river but we could **not** find the entrance. We climbed towards it along a fence, under the cool, green trees, seeing no signs of life save grazing cows and a family of chickens. Each gate bore a sign saying *Défense d'entrer*,[3] which made us more and more determined as it looked so enticing on the other side. Finally we pushed open a forbidden portal and tiptoed into the grounds, feeling deliciously guilty, like spies, or maybe Robin Hoods, sneaking up on the castle from behind. The gleaming towers are a fairy-white and we kept expecting to see a troupe of ladies and knights astride white chargers come trotting down the lowered drawbridge.

By now several tourists had approached from another direction (the official entrance, no doubt) so we walked boldly into the courtyard and joined them. Chaumont was built originally as a fortress and was later swapped for Chenonceaux by Catherine de Médicis, the old tyrant of a queen, thus forcing Diane de Poitiers (the King's favourite) out of Chenonceaux and into Chaumont. Diane disdained the 'gift' and took up residence elsewhere. I wouldn't have if I'd been she. Still, to live in a château with 'C' for 'Catherine' embossed all over it would be a bit disturbing.

Leaving the ghosts of Catherine and Diane, we went on to Amboise, getting there around 4:30 PM. This château is undergoing repairs as it was badly damaged during the German occupation and the scaffolding rather spoils the effect. It is massive and dates from the Middle Ages. We sat down at a café across the river from the château before crossing the bridge to visit it, and ordered lemonades. At the bridge, two *policiers* armed to the teeth were stopping every car. By luck, one of them took a break for a drink at our café and, by eavesdropping on his conversation, we learned that two *condamnés à mort*[4] had escaped from a nearby penitentiary, stolen a car at Richelieu and were in the region 'somewhere'. Nice to know, since we're hitch-hiking!

We'd hoped to get to Chenonceaux before nightfall but it was late by the time we'd finished inspecting the castle; the two *condamnés à mort* were doubtless still circulating in their stolen vehicle; and all in all it seemed a delightful plan to sleep at Amboise. We had supper in a hotel and retired to our room.

> *From a letter to Duncan, dated June 27..................*
> *...two escaped convicts were on the loose in the district in a stolen*
> *car. They'd been condemned to death for making sausages and pâté*
> *out of dead Germans during the war (ugh!)...aren't you glad you*
> *didn't have to defend them in court? Well, we're glad we didn't*
> *happen to thumb a ride with them. I don't fancy ending up on*
> *someone's hors d'oeuvres tray, even at La Tour d'Argent!*

In the morning, my tummy felt funny and a bit swollen; nevertheless we hit the road to Chenonceaux, which is an amazing château built right over the Cher river. It's white and tranquil, has a lovely, formal garden and is approached by a long avenue of trees, which form a gothic, vaulted roof, like a cathedral. Once again we were almost the only visitors.

I wasn't feeling so hot by now. We reached Montrichard by noon, bought some indigestion tablets and our lunch and sat down in a field to picnic. I could hardly eat. My stomach was full of gas, it pained terribly at intervals and I began to have diarrhoea. I obviously couldn't go on, so back we trudged to Montrichard and explained to the pharmacien who'd sold us the tablets that it was much more serious. He gave us the name of a doctor and Beth half-carried me to his office. The doc was gruff at first, saying he had all his regular appointments, etc., but finally, and very kindly, poked my tummy a bit, said that it was a severe indigestion, that I was full of gas, that I needed to rest and take some prescription *médicaments*.

Beth was an angel. She found a quiet hotel near the river, bought all the medicines, the doctor wouldn't accept any payment because '*les Canadiens, ce sont nos amis*', the hotel man made us a special price and so did the druggist. Beth put me to bed, plied me with medicine and, after a bit, I diarrhoea'd out all my lunch, dinner and breakfast, went to sleep and didn't waken until the next morning. I was much better if still a little queasy.

After breakfast we set off for Paris and were phenomenally lucky. The first drive took us to Orléans (we had to pass up Cheverney and

Chambord, two really famous châteaux, mourn, mourn) and here we flagged a man who took us all the way to Paris.

Really, whenever there's an emergency, people are extra nice. And I'm happy I can now talk fluently to French citizens in their own language. I've met many wonderful people during these hitch-hiking tours. Even getting sick was worthwhile in that respect—and it wasn't a total washout for Beth,[5] either, because she went exploring while I was in bed and found a dungeon where Richard the Lion Heart was supposedly imprisoned for nine years, which is why the town is called Montrichard.

MONDAY

Today I'm semi-hysterical, I suppose it's because things are happening so rapidly and my life here is coming to an end. I paid my trunk and train fares today, drew and cashed all my money into dollars (retaining a few francs) and packed the trunk. On top of everything, a strike of the entire French mail, rail and métro system is forecast for July 1—my departure date! The Franconia didn't sail Friday (another strike) but the Mauretania did sail this morning so I'm chewing my cuticles and just hoping. Poor Nancy! She's continually finding that being Grown Up means taking things in one's stride instead of buckling under them.

"NUITS de SCEAUX"

Yesterday afternoon at Sceaux I spent one of my most delightful afternoons since coming to France, all dressed up in my blue silky dress plus perfume—and TWO escorts, John Clark[6] and Jacques. The concert was lovely. Imagine sitting outdoors around the seventeenth century *Pavillon de l'Aube*, listening to the strains of a clavicord and the sweet voice of a singer. We were transported back three centuries in time.

While at Sceaux, the three of us met a Canadian chap from Vancouver, one of the refugees from the beached Franconia. He'd been in Greece, he said, and was simply thrilled in Athens 'by all those Roman ruins'.

I sincerely hope to see you all on July 10. Keep your eye on the newspaper because I may not be able to contact you should the strike materialize. Oh, surely the boat will sail! Ah, France!

All my love, Nancy

[1] a popular laundry powder [2] The staircase of François I
[3] No entry [4] condemned to death
[5] Beth joined the British Foreign Service and served in London, Argentina and Munich, where she held the rank of Consul, the first woman so honoured. She was awarded the OBE in 1982. We wrote and visited until her death in 2007.
[6] John Clark returned to Canada in 1957 and taught at the University of Manitoba, retiring as Head of Modern Languages in 1992.

June 28

Dear Daddy:

Last night I dreamed I looked out the upstairs bathroom window of our house in Halifax; and on the street was an enormous moose, lying down. People were urging it to get up, which it did, picked its way slowly across the road, crossed to our sidewalk and began to smooth out a resting place in our garden...I guess I'm coming home! I promise not to lie down on the plants, though.

Could you buy a crash helmet in preparation for giving me a few catch-up lessons on the car? My driving must be pretty rusty by now.

And I warn you, I'll be taking two tub baths every day.

Bushels of love,
Nancy

packing to leave

P.S. (My hand is shaking so, I can't write properly.)

Dear Family:

> 'Tis Dominion Day,
> 'Tis also parting day.
> No strike,
> Hooray!

It's gorgeous weather out—blue sky and sun. I'm packed, calm (well, relatively calm) and waiting.

Beth Ogilvie, Jacques and Monique will go to the train station with me this afternoon—Nicole and Nouhé are meeting us there.

Friends are wonderful.
I'm too excited to write more.
Hyah ah comes!!!!
I'll phone from Québec.

> Love, N.

Cunard RMS "Samaria"

CERTIFICAT DE FRANÇAIS LITTÉRAIRE

DÉLIVRÉ PAR

L'ÉCOLE SUPÉRIEURE DE PRÉPARATION ET DE PERFECTIONNEMENT
DES PROFESSEURS DE FRANÇAIS A L'ÉTRANGER
FACULTÉ DES LETTRES

Monsieur *Wickwire* Nancy Brown

APRÈS AVOIR SUIVI LE **COURS SUPÉRIEUR DE LANGUE FRANÇAISE** ORGANISÉ PAR L'ÉCOLE SUPÉRIEURE DE PRÉPARATION ET DE PERFECTIONNEMENT DES PROFESSEURS DE FRANÇAIS A L'ÉTRANGER, ET APRÈS AVOIR SUBI AVEC SUCCÈS LES ÉPREUVES DE FIN D'ÉTUDES DE CE COURS ET DU COURS DE PRONONCIATION DE L'**INSTITUT DE PHONÉTIQUE**, A ÉTÉ JUGÉ DIGNE DU

CERTIFICAT DE FRANÇAIS LITTÉRAIRE

Monsieur *Wickwire* AYANT SUIVI LES COURS DE LITTÉRATURE FRANÇAISE, HISTOIRE DE FRANCE, HISTOIRE DE L'ART FRANÇAIS, GÉOGRAPHIE DE LA FRANCE, A SUBI AVEC SUCCÈS L'EXAMEN CONFÉRANT LA

MENTION CULTURE CLASSIQUE

FAIT A PARIS, EN SORBONNE, LE 30 Juin 1955   Mention : Bien.

LE DIRECTEUR :

LES MEMBRES DU JURY :   LE DOYEN :

RÉPUBLIQUE FRANÇAISE — UNIVERSITÉ DE PARIS

INSTITUT DE PHONÉTIQUE

Certificat d'études pratiques de prononciation française

Nous, Doyen de la Faculté des Lettres et Directeur de l'Institut de Phonétique,

Vu la délibération du Conseil de l'Université en date du 28 Mai 1927, approuvée par l'Arrêté ministériel du 11 août 1927,

Vu le Décret du 11 août 1927,

Vu les pièces produites constatant que M lle *Wickwire Nancy* née à *Wolfville* le *24 Juillet* 1934, a rempli les conditions requises et subi l'examen réglementaire à la date du *28 février 1955*

L'avons déclaré digne du *Certificat d'études pratiques de prononciation française*

Fait en Sorbonne, le *28 février 1955*

LE DOYEN,   LE DIRECTEUR DE L'INSTITUT,

Nous, Recteur, Président du Conseil de l'Université, visons le présent Certificat, que nous délivrons à M lle *Wickwire Nancy*

Paris, le 5 JUIL 1955   19

Signature du Titulaire,   LE RECTEUR,

Paris, I.A.C. 8 rue de Fürstenberg

The University of Paris awarded these two magnificent certificates.

EPILOGUE

And Then What?

I returned to Halifax on July 10, 1955 and was appalled by what seemed its obscene materialism, symbolized by the new auto models with their huge, Crayola-hued fins. Got over that, earned a Nova Scotia Teacher's Certificate and taught French at Queen Elizabeth High School, where five years earlier (I was proud of this) I'd been a student. Duncan and I married and moved to Brockville, Ontario. He had been accepted into a law firm. I was not so lucky. In Upper Canada, Sorbonne or no Sorbonne, I was *persona non grata* without an Ontario Teacher's Certificate.

So, I threw myself into community theatre, brought up a son and daughter and finally, after Queen's University in nearby Kingston opened a Faculty of Education, enrolled in order to meet the Ontario requirements—landing a French teaching job immediately. By the 1970s, the 'sit still and memorize the vocabulary list' method was obsolete. We—pupils and teacher—sang and acted our way through the French lessons. There was a hair in the soup, though. After two decades in an anglophone environment, French-speaking skills can become clumsy. This flaw was attacked by enrolling in summer vacation French courses at French or Swiss universities, beginning with Grenoble in 1977. Tuition was reimbursed by the Ontario government, about whose teacher qualification policy I ceased to grumble.

All this led to my being named French consultant for the Leeds and Grenville County Board of Education. My old Dalhousie professor, Paul Chavy, was delighted. In 1988-89 I inaugurated a French immersion program for the Board, moved in 1989-90 to Queen's University Faculty of Education as Adjunct Professor of French and retired in 2002 to prepare a long-delayed Master of Arts degree.

Paul Chavy died in 2003, aged 89.

Letters from Paris is dedicated to his memory.

Postscript

J uly 1979 found me at the University of Tours. Much had changed since 1955. No more ocean voyages for starters—everyone flew to Paris. The new generation of French citizens was taller by a head than their forbears. 'Slacks', thought disreputable in the 50s, were the Western woman's everyday wear. Charles De Gaulle established the stable Fifth Republic in 1958, followed in 1960 by a currency revaluation: thereafter one *nouveau franc*, new franc, replaced 100 *anciens francs*. After the student riots of 1968, *la réforme de l'éducation* loosened the stays of France's old-fashioned, authoritarian system. Though on a student budget when it came to dorms and meals, I could eschew hitchhiking and travel First Class, thanks to a French Rail Pass purchased in Canada. Still, there were reassuring echos of 1954, a case of *plus ça change...*

Many hotel rooms, for example, had no toilets, tubs or showers and certainly no soap. Business opening and closing hours remained engagingly unpredictable. Waiters and shop clerks greeted the tiniest errors in French pronunciation with feigned incomprehension ('*Hein? Comment?*') Lotharios still chatted up solo women and university exam procedures remained preserved in amber.

One letter from the 1976-1988 'summer study abroad' period, addressed to my 17-year old daughter Elspeth and dated July 23, 1979, is reproduced as a postscript on the following pages.

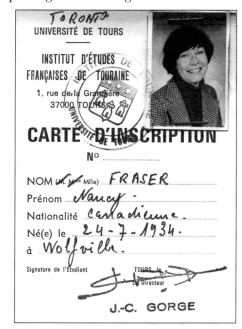

Dear Elspeth:

I really must record my pilgrimage to La Rochelle and Poitiers before time erases details.

Sandals and an overnight bag containing pyjamas, camera, toothbrush and a lunch of cheese, cherries and a hard-boiled egg were the ideal travel companions. Oh, and a fresh *petit pain* bought just before boarding the train.

It is boring to sit in silence in First Class, where the chairs face each other like CNR First Class. A very elegant French woman sat opposite me, surely a Parisienne, stunning grey tweed suit and hair in a chic chignon. I, though inelegant in sweater and trousers, plucked up courage and asked if she would 'accept' to chat. (*'Accepteriez-vous de bavarder un petit peu avec moi?'*) She accepted, if a bit taken aback, but relaxed when she discovered I was a *professeur* whose *mari* was an *avocat*—prestigious professions both, in France.

Twelve noon. La Rochelle! I swung off the train to a lovely sea smell and a surprise: the tourist bureau was nowhere near the *gare* (usually there is one *juste en face*). So I hoofed it a good two miles past the *vieux port* and up narrow streets with sidewalks eight inches wide, dodging *vélos* and Renaults, and finally arrived at the *Hospitalité*. Here three young women were frantically trying to find hotel rooms for a steady stream of tourists. When my turn came the young woman looked despondent. "*Il n'y a rien*", she insisted, "*pour une personne pour une nuit*".[1] She tried several hotels and received a 'Non' from each. Even if they had rooms, they refused to rent them to a single person, they insisted on two or more. Apparently La Rochelle is the Myrtle Beach of France.

I was getting horribly hungry (it was one-thirty) so I decided to find a Bar-Snack and see if the *patronne* would let me eat my picnic lunch with a glass of her white wine. Ah! A clean-looking Snack with the usual heap of hard-boiled eggs and pile of oranges on the counter

---

[1] There's nothing for one person for one night.

plus little chairs and *guéridons* (pedestal tables). Certainly Madame could eat her lunch here with *un petit verre de blanc*. As I was munching away, in came three or four pals of the patronne. They each had a *verre* and amid much joshing, began boasting of their marital infidelities. Noticing me, one of them asked if I'd verify that he was a chap with *du charme*. I said, sure thing, in fact all Frenchmen were charming. This together with my foreign accent tickled the assembly and they burst spontaneously into song. They insisted on buying me a second glass of *blanc*...we chatted about Canada...and after handshakes all 'round, I went back to the Hospitalité.

Nope. No rooms. Would I care to rent a vélo and stay in a dorm at the Auberge de Jeunesse outside town? No, actually. But *pas de problème*, I'd take the 17:30 train to Poitiers, which I'd intended to visit anyway. Could she telephone to Poitiers for a room? She could and did, at the Tin Plate Hotel, (Hôtel du Plat d'Etain) in the centre of town, 34 francs. Perfect. I paid her the 5 franc fee for locating a room and went off on the *visite commentée en calèche*,[2] which started at 2:30 PM.

Do you remember the sketch of Marie-Antoinette on her way to the guillotine, head shaven, sitting in a wooden wagon like a hay wagon? That's a calèche, ma chère, and ten of us plus a guide climbed into it. It had a bench along each side, two gigantic wheels, a coachman and a very strong bay mare who pulled us. It was tremendous fun. I felt transported to the

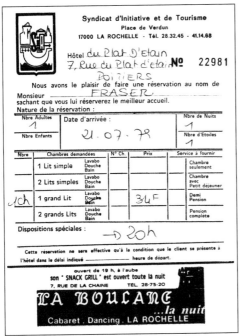

---

[2] guided wagon tour

seventeenth century, nay, the tenth! Bumpy, slow and steady. We sat up so high we could easily see the gargoyles and mediaeval coats of arms on the various houses. La Rochelle was an independent city until Louis XIII (actually his immensely clever and powerful minister, the Cardinal de Richelieu) reduced the city after a starvation siege, during which the population of 20,000 plummeted to 5,000. La Rochelle was protestant and its enterprising population rolled in wealth due to a flourishing trade with England, Germany, Scandinavia and Canada. After the siege, the Protestants were banished and the port never regained its spirit of enterprise. I compared it to Halifax, which faces it across the Atlantic and which is a hundred times more dynamic (and Halifax isn't the liveliest city in North America). One whole street was paved in granite stones from Canada. In the 18th century the fur trade revived La Rochelle a bit; but furs aren't heavy enough to provide sufficient ballast, so blocks of granite were added. The granite was used to pave streets and build houses.

After the *visite commentée*, which was excellent, I stumped back to the station and boarded the train. Off to Poitiers, a city whose name evokes battle after battle, from the seventh century to the Hundred Years' War. I arrived about 6:30 PM and faced a terrific climb up a set of steps steeper than Sacré-Coeur in Montmartre, then more hiking, ever upwards to the *centre ville*, where the Hôtel de Ville, an imposing Renaissance structure, watches over a large, open square bordered by small café-bars, shops and cinémas. The rue du Plat d'Etain was just behind the principal cinéma and sure enough, they were expecting me. The clerk produced a mammoth key attached to a wooden plaque, Room Number 8. It had a double bed, wardrobe, wash basin, bidet and two towels but (I'd forgotten about this) NO SOAP. And it was nearly seven o'clock, shop closing time. I dashed to the pharmacie across the street, having also forgotten to pack Vaseline to remove my makeup. Well!

First, they pretended they'd never heard of petroleum jelly and tried to sell me some *lait démaquillant*[3] by Lancôme. Finally, with a world of contempt, they brought out a tube of petroleum jelly labelled in four languages. "*Si vous voulez vous démaquiller avec ÇA* (great emphasis on the *ça*)...*alors...*»[4] words failed him. Certainly I was prepared to démaquiller with THAT, now did they have some *savon*, not too dear? They proposed a soap elegantly packaged in floral paper by Christian Dior. *Ah, non. Merci quand même.* I went out followed by disdainful looks and began a search for soap. Sure enough, in a little sort of 7/11 shop I bought a cake of Palmolive for one franc 50 centimes. The vendeuse offered, in change (and this is the only place in France, either in 1977 or 1979 I've seen this), **old francs**. Two *anciens francs* are worth two centimes today. And the re-valuation was in 1960! She gave me five ancient francs as she had no 5-centime coins.

Poitiers is a *ville morte*.[5] At 7:00 PM everything shuts. No one even eats out, apparently, as there was not a restaurant open: **FERMETURE ANNUELLE 15 JUILLET—15 AOUT**[6] was in every window. I ended up at the Hôtel de France which proposed a menu at 40 francs, *taxe et service compris*. A bit more expensive than I'd planned but with care I could just manage. A deathly silence reigned. Beyond great glass doors was the dining room in which eight waiters, superb in white jackets, waited. A venerable maître d', about five feet tall and bald as a spoon, pretended to be busy behind a desk.

As I marched towards the glass portals everyone inside stood to attention. A customer! I was seated beside the cash register. *Merci,* (pointing) *je préfère cette table-là. Très bien, Madame.* I chose the 40-franc menu and a tiny bottle of wine for 10 francs. The waiter uncorked it importantly. First course, *salade Hôtel de France.* By now two couples, consisting each of a creaking old gentleman and his wife, also old but terrifically well-maintained and restored, like the old buildings, had entered. The same large bowl of salad was wheeled from table to table

---

[3] makeup remover

[4] If you want to remove your makeup with THAT...well...

[5] ghost town

[6] Annual closing - July 15 to August 15

and, French service of course, one was served by the waiters who by now were in a flutter because a few more customers had arrived and they could go into their well-rehearsed waiter act.

We were served judiciously tiny portions of egg and tomato on somewhat larger pieces of lettuce. Next the *plat principal*, which was *jambon du pays* and *ratatouille*. An enormous, antique serving table on wheels with a great silver platter on top, the kind with a hinged cover that folds back and spirit lamps underneath, arrived from the kitchen. We all held our breath. Underneath this ducal covering was THE HAM. Everyone was having ham. The waiter served my neighbour, an elderly lady. Next, my turn. Two of the thinnest slices of *jambon* imaginable were expertly removed from the haunch and with every flourish, arranged on my plate. A dollop of ratatouille was added and voilà. There wasn't enough meat to satisfy a single wasp but the whole thing was so comic, it was worth it. Besides I knew I could defeat them at dessert which was **either** cheese **or** ice cream. I chose cheese and when the platter arrived, requested some of each of four kinds. They were stuck, they had to give it to me and that way I got enough to eat after all.

After the repast, I walked back to the town square and sat upon a bench near a very small girl named Sabine, who had a doll in a carry-all bed. Sabine took no notice of my accent nor the fact that I could have been a baby-snatcher. "*Je vais m'asseoir à côté de toi*",[7] she announced comfortably. She had an Eskimo pie on a stick and was consuming it delightedly. We chatted for a good half-hour, during which she said her mother was a *professeur* and taught English in Spain. Eventually her papa came to get her (he'd been having a coffee all this time on a terrace) and as I took my leave, a young woman rushed up breathless and said, "*O, Michel, je te cherchais partout*" to the man. I said, "*Je dois dire que votre petite fille est charmante*".[8] (The *charmante* Sabine was by now having a tiny tantrum because bedtime loomed.) "*Oh*", said the

---

[7] I'm going to sit beside you.

[8] Oh, Michel, I've been looking for you everywhere...I must say your little girl is charming ....

160

woman, a bit flustered, *'je ne suis pas sa mère…enfin…"* [9] and I knew I'd put my foot in it.

I excused myself and went, soap and Vaseline in hand, back to the Tin Plate hotel. Slept well, too. And breakfast was superb: croissants hot from the baker and fresh, delicious coffee. Then, off to the *visite commentée* which began in front of the most celebrated monument in Poitiers, the Cathédrale de Ste. Marie-la-Grande. The cathedral is a celebrated example of romanesque architecture with a superb façade dating from the eleventh century. The interior was so stirring, as I walked along the left aisle it seemed I was standing still and the church was moving towards me. The romanesque churches are much more meaningful than the gothic ones, which are immense, full of sculptures and stained glass and bleeding Christs and gilded Virgins, cold, high vaulted ceilings, etc.

église gothique   *église romane*   *église mérovingienne*

There were only four of us on the tour which was relaxed and nice. We saw all the remarkable romanesque churches and finally, a tiny, merovingian church from the seventh century; really, this did make my throat catch. Tiny little windows, inexpertly-chiselled primitive decorations, thick, thick stone walls. Underneath one can just glimpse the foundations of a Roman villa on which the church was built.

---

[9] Oh… I'm not her mother…actually…..

By noon I felt like a real pilgrim, plus I knew I'd better get some food before the shops closed. Poitiers showed its *ville morte* character again: unlike everywhere else in France where the charcuteries, épiceries and pâtisseries are open Sunday until twelve-thirty or one o'clock, everything was bolted and the big shutters locked. I didn't have enough money left for a restaurant. Finally I found a fruit store open and got a peach and a banana, figuring that would do. On the way back to the *gare* I perceived a woman with a baguette. Holà! This was like the dove bringing Noah the olive branch. Somewhere, a shop must be open. Sure enough, an épicerie run by the usual thick-set, middle-aged couple dispensed cheese. I bought a slice of Bonbel, had lunch on a bench in an exquisite, deserted public garden...and three kilometers later, reached the gare. It was only two o'clock, the train left at three-thirty but I was happy to sink into a restaurant chair with a cup of café-crème and a magazine until train time.

At 4:30 PM I was in Tours, at 5:15 back at the university résidence, having with difficulty brushed off a lanky Senegalese gentleman, black as coal and with bad teeth, who decided I was the creature of his dreams. Could he invite me for *un petit café*? *Merci, non.* He boarded the bus with me and we chatted. He is studying law at Tours (he said). I was *tellement sympathique.* Could he perhaps show me his student apartment? Thank you, very kind, *très gentil* but no thanks. Maybe I'd do him the honour of coming to lunch *chez lui*? The fact that my husband would join me within the week deterred him not a whit. Could he accompany me to my room? By now I was laughing merrily (ridicule, the ultimate anti-aphrodisiac) and he got the picture, 'remembered' an engagement and descended at the next stop.

It's ten o'clock – I must shower, shampoo and go to bed. Final exams tomorrow.

Monday, July 23rd

Ouf! Today those of us who so chose, sat two examinations: in the morning, a dictation (*dictée*), in the afternoon, a composition. We had an hour for the first, three hours for the second and incredible as it seems, we needed them. The organization of the first exam was marvelously French. To begin with, the exam room could not be entered as the lights refused to 'march'. Two hundred students waited jammed in a narrow hallway while this was fixed. We then all piled in and sat down in an arrangement of chairs and long tables which I shall have to sketch. Whether this disposition of furniture has been handed

down from the time of Charlemagne and is therefore sacrosanct, I know not. Everyone was seated; I took seat A on the diagram. At this point a dear little old man, garbed for the ceremony in a clean brown lab-coat with matching checked shirt and tie, appeared with a packet of little papers and some Scotch tape. Beginning at the professor's left he began gumming the papers onto the tables. You have guessed it. The papers contained our names, numbers and nationalities. A huge rearrangement of bodies now began, as each person tried to find where he/she was supposed to sit. This entailed considerable delay. I ended up at place B on the plan. When everyone was finally settled, the professeur came in and walked along every aisle checking the names again. The French are maniacs when it comes to 'contrôle'. We had all pre-registered for the exam, so why? *Vive la France!* This must be why France is no longer a World Power. The *dictée* was full of traps, doubtless I fell into some of them.

The afternoon saw us all gamely back for the composition (*thème*). We had a choice among three subjects: I chose: 'It is said that children's toys are designed to create little programmed adults.

Discuss.' By 5:15 PM I was still correcting (we were allowed dictionaries) but had to hand in the copy. What a feeling of relief to swing out into the sunshine and practically RUN for the bus! As a reward I'll have the one franc fifty special—a miniature bottle of wine—with my cafeteria supper tonight.

Love, Mum

'The one franc fifty special'

Acknowledgements

My grateful thanks to my husband Duncan and Dr. Peter Waite for editorial advice, Jean Boyd and John Waddington for computer instruction, Marcelle Vandendries, Marie-Hélène Bouillot and Duncan for merciless proof-reading, John Clark, Tui Flower, Sture Jansson and Ben Westerbeek for verification of anecdotes and Stephanie Hussey and Lee Stover of Henderson Printing, for their good-humoured patience.

I wish also to thank those former students, and/or their families, who agreed to appear in the book.

A few names have been changed.

All sketches and photographs are by the author
unless otherwise identified.

By the same author:
Mysterious Brockville   2000
Mysterious Brockville 2   2006